The
Paths
of
Poetry

The Paths of Poetry

TWENTY-FIVE POETS AND THEIR POEMS

Louis Untermeyer

DELACORTE PRESS

NEW YORK

ILLUSTRATED BY *Ellen Raskin*

ESPECIALLY FOR

Lynn AND *Lee*

CONTENTS

WHAT IS POETRY?

Poetry is the record of the best and happiest moments of the happiest and best minds.

PERCY BYSSHE SHELLEY

Poetry is the art of uniting pleasure with truth by calling imagination to the help of reason. . . . The essence of poetry is invention, such invention as, by producing something unexpected, surprises and delights.

SAMUEL JOHNSON

Poetry teaches the enormous force of a few words.

RALPH WALDO EMERSON

Poetry should strike the reader as a wording of his own highest thoughts, and appear almost a remembrance.

JOHN KEATS

Poetry is simply the most beautiful, impressive, and widely effective mode of saying things.

MATTHEW ARNOLD

Poetry is not the assertion that something is true, but the making of that truth more fully real to us.

T. S. ELIOT

The right reader of a good poem can tell the moment it strikes him that he will never get over it. That is to say, permanence in poetry as in love is perceived instantly. It hasn't to await the test of time.

ROBERT FROST

There is a light upon the poets, especially upon the Elizabethans
and Keats, Wordsworth, Coleridge, Shelley. These are the
people with whom I want to live, these are the men I feel
are our brothers.

KATHERINE MANSFIELD

Poetry's power is the magic of expressing the inexpressible—
and expressing it in terms of the unforgettable.

MICHAEL LEWIS

What is a poet? To whom does he address himself? He is a man
speaking to men . . . a man who rejoices more than other
men in the spirit of life that is in him.

WILLIAM WORDSWORTH

A FOREWORD

There is no frigate like a book
To take us lands away,
Nor any courser like a page
Of prancing poetry.

That is the way Emily Dickinson described her pleasure in reading, especially in reading a book of poetry. She compared her delight to the sensation of sailing to far-off countries on a swift boat or galloping happily on the back of some spirited steed.

To Keats, poetry was exciting in a more exalted way. He felt it as

a drainless shower of light. . . .
'Tis the supreme of power,
'Tis might half slumbering on its own right arm.

Every writer, as well as every reader, has had a different definition of poetry. To Shakespeare it was "a golden cadence . . . heaven-bred." Wordsworth said it was "the spontaneous overflow of powerful feelings . . . the breath and finer spirit of all knowledge." Shelley believed the power of words was so great that "poets are the unacknowledged legislators of the world." Pope added that nations could not hope to survive without poetry:

Vain was the chief's, the sage's pride;
They had no poet, and they died.

13

This book is an account of twenty-five of these "unacknowl-edged legislators," music-makers, "movers and shakers," poets who have influenced our ideas, affected our emotions and enriched our language. The chapters not only tell the stories of their lives but also relate the lives to their poems and reveal how and why they wrote the way they did. The book aims to show what the poets meant to the development of literature and, most of all, what they mean to us.

The
Paths
of
Poetry

Founder of English Literature

GEOFFREY CHAUCER
[1340?–1400]

WE TEND too often to think of the poet as a daydreamer, incompetent and eccentric, an irresponsible creature trying to escape reality. But, with few exceptions, poets have been not only dreamers but doers, men of action occupied with everyday life and busy with affairs of the world.

Besides being author of the grandest epic in our language, Milton was an important official who prepared propaganda for a rebel government, a courageous fighter who opposed the "divine right" of kings.

Shakespeare was no less the world's greatest dramatist for being a successful businessman.

Sir Walter Raleigh was a dozen men in one: soldier, sailor, historian, member of Parliament, adventurer, explorer who prospected for gold in Guiana when South America was just beginning to be known, and founder of the colony which, in honor of Elizabeth, the Virgin Queen, was named Virginia.

Sir Philip Sidney was a soldier who became a heroic symbol.

Until he learned how to write plays, Ben Jonson was a bricklayer.

Robert Herrick began his working life as a manufacturing jeweler.

17

William Blake not only designed and printed his books but sold them himself.

Lord Byron lost his life in an attempt to liberate the Greeks from Turkish tyranny.

Walt Whitman gave up a career as journalist to devote himself to wounded veterans hospitalized during the Civil War.

Robert Burns and Robert Frost were hardworking farmers.

Geoffrey Chaucer, called "the father of English poetry and perhaps the prince of it," was controller of customs in London and agent for his country on important diplomatic missions abroad.

The date of Chaucer's birth is uncertain; it is presumed to have been sometime in 1340. His father, John Chaucer, was a wine merchant who had done so well that he had attained some connection with the royal household; he was one of those who accompanied King Edward III on a state journey to Germany. John Chaucer's house was close to the Thames, and young Geoffrey spent much of his time with other boys along the riverside, watching the ships load and unload their cargoes, fascinated by the looks of men and merchandise from all over the world. In school, besides studying Latin, he learned French, for French was the language of commerce as well as that of the court. But his speech was the Midland dialect, or Middle English, which was spoken in London and which he was the first to turn into literature.

The boy grew up in a violent century, a century riddled with wars between France and England, intermittent truces, terrible plagues, and a bloody peasants' revolt. The Hundred Years' War had broken out a few years before he was born. Chaucer was six years old when the English archers, using the longbows they had perfected, defeated the patrician horsemen of France and won a great victory at the battle of Crécy. A year later he heard about another English triumph: the occupation of Calais, which, after a long siege, fell to the English artillery. He was among the thousands who waited for hours for the return of the conquerors, cheered the yeoman, the sturdy longbowmen, even louder than the knights, and who shouted to one another in a happy comradeship.

The fourteenth century was also a period of exciting creation. History was being not only made but written about. Songs celebrating victories and lusty ballads about Robin Hood were being composed; poets were made welcome at private palaces as well as at royal courts. And at court Geoffrey Chaucer, while still in his teens, was a young attendant. He was part of the household of the Countess of Ulster; a book of records shows that the countess had bought him a handsome livery: a fashionable red cloak and a pair of tight-fitting black-and-red breeches.

Young Chaucer was already well equipped to consort with educated aristocrats. He had excelled in his studies, which included music as well as mathematics, grammar wrapped up in moral maxims, religion, astronomy and astrology, a foretelling of the future by studying the positions of the planets and their influence on human affairs, a pseudo-science in which Chaucer's contemporaries believed. Reading was a passion with him. He read everything he could find anywhere. He could never get enough of the storytellers, chiefly the Latin ones and especially Ovid, whose romances were dear to the heart of the growing boy and whose tales he was to retell later in his own way.

After serving two years with the Countess of Ulster, who became Duchess of Clarence as the result of her marriage to the son of King Edward III, Chaucer had his first taste of warfare. It was not a glorious experience. Battles were as often lost as won on French soil; deals were constantly made between the victors and the vanquished; as much profit was gained by ransom as by the occupation of territory. Chaucer was thrown in with mercenaries, soldiers of fortune, ruffian adventurers; he got to know the ignoble as well as the noble features of life. During the siege of Rheims he was taken prisoner and, after the bargaining which was part of the usual business of war, was released upon payment of sixteen pounds. His ransom was paid by the Keeper of the King's Wardrobe.

Upon his return to England Chaucer became a member of the king's household; his royal master referred to him as "our very dear valet" and gave him a pension for life. (The king's valet was not, as the term ordinarily implies, a servant who lays out clothes and helps dress his employer, but a person of rank, a diplomat, a close companion, and, at times, a confidential agent.) Chaucer soon attained eminent rank. He was sent abroad to military conferences and on the king's private affairs. He was still in his twenties when he married Philippa Roet, whose sister was the third wife of the prominent John of Gaunt, one of the most powerful men in the country. With John of Gaunt's patronage and the king's favor, Chaucer's future seemed assured.

Chaucer's marriage was a contented if not a romantic one. His wife bore him two sons—he refers to one of them fondly as "little Lewis"—and, although the record is not clear about this, there seem to have been two daughters. We know nothing of Philippa's character, and we should not confuse an author's private life with his public writings; but in Chaucer's poems it is usually the wife rather than the husband who is strong-willed, independent, and victorious in all arguments.

Whether or not Chaucer was lord of his household, he was unquestionably successful as a diplomat. He was still in his twenties when he was sent abroad on new missions. He made at least two trips to Italy, where he discovered the great Italian writers of the period. Dante, a politician as well as a poet, was dead, but Boccaccio was lecturing on Dante's *The Divine Comedy* and speaking about it in his native tongue instead of in Latin, which had always been used for discussion of the classics. It is more than likely that this innovation gave Chaucer the desire not only to write but also to write in the common speech of the people rather than in the classical language of the scholars. Moreover, had Chaucer not become acquainted with the stories in Boccaccio's lively *Decameron*, he might never have written his narrative masterpiece, *The Canterbury Tales*.

By the time Chaucer returned to England, he had collected scores of stories and was beginning to tell them in a new kind of verse. However, it was not for his poetry but for his excellent services as emissary that he was rewarded with an important position: Controller of Customs for the Port of London. The salary was high, and he was able to buy a large house of his own. He was also presented with another life pension.

In appearance Chaucer did not resemble the romantic picture
of the dreamy poet with striking features, alabaster brow, and
eyes "in a fine frenzy rolling." We have no portraits of Chaucer
painted during his lifetime, but a miniature made shortly after
his death gives him a serious, slightly worried look, small quiz-
zical eyes, a thin mouth, and a scraggy beard. He did not prettify
himself in his writings. He wanted his readers to know exactly
what he felt, what he loved, what he despised, what he considered remarkable or ridiculous. He never spared himself. He
seems to have been shy, a poor talker—the Countess of Pem-
broke said his silence was more enjoyable than his speech—and
he made fun of his own dullness in public. In *The Canterbury
Tales* he lets one of the characters, the host, joke about his
stoutness, his serious manner, his abstract air, his puckish
expression, and his way of wandering away from the subject.
Chaucer makes the host, whom Chaucer has appointed a sort
of master of ceremonies, describe the poet in these teasing terms:

Who is this man with such a curious air,
Searching the ground as if to spot a hare!
Come closer, man, and look up fearlessly.
Make room, good sirs, for he deserves a place.
Look at him with an ample waist like me,
But puppet-like, little and fair of face,
Fit for a woman's tenderest embrace.
Yet, though he looks and acts like some strange elf,
He keeps himself severely to himself.

In his mid-thirties Chaucer was given another opportunity
to show how good a diplomat he was. He was again sent abroad,
this time to help negotiate a treaty between England and Italy.
It was a difficult mission, for the powerful group in Milan,
headed by the Visconti brothers, was suspected of criminal
activities as well as treachery. But Chaucer conducted the mili-
tary-financial arrangements with great skill and was honored by
both parties to the amicable agreement. His task was made more
enjoyable because the Viscontis were patrons of art and literature; their palace had been decorated by Giotto and the library
was full of treasures by Dante, Petrarch, and Boccaccio. A

renewed acquaintance with these great poets and storytellers enabled Chaucer to act as a conductor of two cultures between two different civilizations.

Meanwhile Chaucer continued to search for his own way of writing. He had been born with the gift of rhyming and image-making; he had learned the importance of small but significant details. In his mid-twenties he improved his technique by trans-lating "The Romance of the Rose," a popular French poem of the period. A few years later he made his debut as an original poet with *The Book of the Duchess,* an allegory that was also an elegy on the death of the first wife of his patron, John of Gaunt.

In this poem Chaucer found he could make his own music. He did it by combining the sounds of the everyday language spoken by his countrymen with the rhythms and accents used by the French poets, such as pronouncing the letter *e* at the end of a word like "rote" (root) or "sote" (sweet), making it an extra syllable, as is still the custom when reciting French verse. At forty he elaborated on the allegorical pattern with *The House of Fame,* a bird-and-beast fable in which the most amus-ing parts are the occasional "asides." It is more than likely that Chaucer was referring to his wife when he declares that the eagle's cry may be piercing but it is softer than the voice that wakes him every morning.

His next work, *The Parliament of Fowls,* is more fantastic. It concerns a vast assembly of birds that gather every year to choose their mates—and the great day is, appropriately, St. Valentine's Day. Later, in "The Nun's Priest's Tale" (in *The Canterbury Tales*), Chaucer related one of the loveliest of all bird-and-beast fables, but *The Parliament of Fowls* is delightful, especially in the way Chaucer describes the different charac-teristics of the birds: the "vigilant" goose, the jay strutting in his pride, the raven sure of his wisdom, the crow with his mournful caw, the ducks who, though commonplace, are not impressed by the lordly airs of the more elegantly feathered fowl. We even get a glimpse of Chaucer's struggle with his work. The very first line of the poem declares:

The life so short, the craft so long to learn.

It is sometimes thought that Chaucer buried himself in his books; he himself wrote that he would read until he was dazed. But he had many other things to do. For the Controller of Customs there were accounts to keep, reckonings to be made, people to interview. Moreover, he had a deep love of the outdoors. In the Prologue to *The Legend of Good Women* he tells how he cannot wait for spring so he can roam in the fields, observe the budding flowers—he had a special fondness for the wide-eyed daisy, the "day's eye"—and spend time away from the written word.

> . . . Then, when the month of May
> Comes in, and I can hear the sweet birds sing
> And all the little buds begin to spring,
> Then, such it seems is my condition,
> Farewell my book and my devotion!

Chaucer liked to speak of himself as a hermit, but "his abstinence was little." He was fond of the good things of life. The king's butler had been ordered to present the poet with a pitcher of wine every day; in his fifties the daily pitcher was increased to an annual tun of wine, a cask containing some two hundred and fifty gallons. At forty-six he sat in Parliament as a knight of Kent. Chaucer, it seems, was scarcely the hermit he thought himself.

In his early forties Chaucer began *Troilus and Criseyde,* which has been called the first novel; certainly it is the first novel in verse form. According to the *Iliad* Troilus was one of the sons of Priam, king of Troy, but in Homer's epic there is no mention of the young prince's love for the girl whom Chaucer calls Criseyde. In a legend made up in the Middle Ages she was known as Cressida, and Chaucer borrowed the tale from Boccaccio, as did Shakespeare in his play *Troilus and Cressida.* Borrowing plots was a common practice. Nobody thought the worse of an author for taking a story from some source, usually foreign, and adapting it to his own purpose; it was even a credit to an author, for it showed a wide acquaintance with other literatures besides his own. It was what the author did with his borrowed material that counted.

For *Troilus and Criseyde* Chaucer added situations and invented characters—Pandarus, for example, was Chaucer's own creation, a comic figure whom Shakespeare turned into an immoral go-between. This great work of fiction was further distinguished by being written in stanzas of seven lines, "rhyme royal," which became known as "the Chaucer stanza." This, in modern English, is an illustration of the form:

> Now Troilus looked straight at her, and found
> How pleasant were her features and how dear.
> While she—she kept her eyes upon the ground
> Except for just one glance which, without fear,
> Implied she, too, had reason to be here.
> The glance was quick, but very warm and bright.
> Young Troilus observed it with delight.

Chaucer was now ready to write his immortal work, *The Canterbury Tales*. It took him ten or twelve years to write, and it remained unfinished. It was an extremely ambitious project. Chaucer imagined a group pilgrimage to the shrine of Thomas à Becket at Canterbury—it is possible that he himself had gone on such a pilgrimage—and the group consisted of thirty pilgrims. The journey was to be enlivened with storytelling. Each pilgrim was supposed to tell four tales—two on the trip down, two more on the way back—but Chaucer lived to complete only twenty-three of the planned one hundred and twenty. Nevertheless, the story-poems are, as Dryden said, three hundred years later, "a perpetual fountain of good sense," filled with "God's plenty." All of fourteenth-century English life, its gaiety, its grimness, and its tremendous gusto, is in them.

The Canterbury Tales begins with a Prologue, one of the loveliest celebrations of spring ever written. Here are the early rain-fresh flowers, the sweet breath of the west wind, the small birds singing from every bough, and the warm air waking in every breast the desire to leave the house and journey forth.

This is the way the Prologue opens in Chaucer's own language:

Whan that Aprille with his shoures sote
The droghte of Marche hath perced to the rote,
And bathed every veyne in swich licour
Of which vertu engendred is the flour:
Whan Zephirus eek with his swete breeth
Inspired hath in every holt and heeth
The tendre croppes, and the yonge sonne
Hath in the Ram his halfe cours y-ronne,
And smale fowles maken melodye
That slepen al the night with open yë
(So priketh hem nature in hir corages):
Than longen folk to goon on pilgrimages,
And palmers for to seken straunge strondes,
To ferne halwes couthe in sondry londes;
And specially, from every shires ende
Of Engelond, to Caunterbury they wende
The holy blisful martir for to seke
That hem hath holpen, whan that they were seke.

To appreciate the subtlety and to derive full enjoyment of
the rich music of Chaucer's verse, it should be read in the
original. But this presents a difficulty to those untrained in an
understanding of fourteenth-century Middle English. For the
convenience of readers who find it too great an obstacle, the
poetry in this chapter appears in my own modern English version. The following is an adaptation of that part of the Prologue
just quoted.

When the sweet showers of April follow March,
Piercing the dryness to the roots that parch,
Bathing each vein in such a flow of power
That a new strength's engendered in the flower—
When, with a gentle warmth, the west-wind's breath
Awakes in every wood and barren heath
The tender foliage; when the vernal sun
Has half his course within the Ram to run;

When the small birds are making melodies,
Sleeping all night (they say) with open eyes
(For Nature so within their bosom rages)—
Then people long to go on pilgrimages,
And palmers wander to the strangest strands
For famous shrines, however far the lands.
Especially from every shire's end
Of England's length to Canterbury they wend,
Seeking the martyr, holiest and blest
Who helped them, healed their ills, and gave them rest.

Each member of the pilgrim group is sharply individualized. The host, a large, rough, good-natured fellow, is worthy to have been "a marshal in a hall." A knight, bold in battle, has the meekness of a maid, "a truly perfect, noble knight." His son, the youthful squire, is "a lover and a bachelor" with his curled hair neatly trimmed. There is a monk who is fond of hunting, fine clothes, and rich dishes; "he loved a fat swan best of any roast." A prioress was so coy that her greatest oath was "By Saint Loy!" and her table manners were so dainty that she never dropped a morsel of food or "wet her fingers in the sauce." A friar was particularly popular because he spoke charmingly, played the fiddle, sang, and affected a slight lisp which he thought was attractive. The red-faced, broad-hatted Wife of Bath was a jolly, talkative person who had had five husbands as well as "other company in youth." A stocky, heavy-shouldered miller with a beard as red as a fox excelled at wrestling, playing the bagpipes, and roaring out jokes from a mouth as broad "as a great furnace." A student from Oxford, who seems to have been modeled on Chaucer, loved books rather than fine clothing; he was a man "full of high sentence" and moral values—"and gladly would he learn, and gladly teach."

All the others were described with equal shrewdness and exactness, the little gestures and the large generosities, the very shades of complexion, the mingled virtues and vices. Nothing was omitted; there was nothing that Chaucer could not lift into poetry. His love of life extended to every part of it, not just

the sweetness and serenity, not only the loveliness but its liveli-
ness—everything that was ordinary as well as the extraordinary,
the everyday, the earthy, even the vulgar. Chaucer was a magnificent storyteller, and his narratives combine action and
character, a swiftly moving plot, and a vivid panorama of
personalities. Here are four of the more winning pilgrims:

A KNIGHT

A Knight there was, and that a worthy man,
Who, from the moment when he first began
To ride forth, loved the code of chivalry:
Honor and truth, freedom and courtesy.
His lord's war had established him in worth;
He rode—and no man further—ends of earth
In heathen parts as well as Christendom,
Honored wherever he might go or come . . .
Of mortal battles he had seen fifteen,
And fought hard for our faith at Tramassene
Thrice in the lists, and always slain his foe.
This noble knight was even led to go
To Turkey where he fought most valiantly
Against the heathen hordes for Palaty.
Renowned he was; and, worthy, he was wise.
Prudence, with him, was more than mere disguise;
He was as meek in manner as a maid.
Vileness he shunned, rudeness he never said
In all his life, respecting each man's right.
He was a truly perfect, noble knight.

A SQUIRE

With him there was his son, a youthful squire,
A merry blade, a lover full of fire;
With locks as curled as though laid in a press—
Scarce twenty years of age was he, I guess.
In stature he was of an average length,
Wondrously active, quick, and great in strength.

He proved himself a soldier handsomely
In Flanders, in Artois and Picardy,
Bearing himself so well, in so short space,
Hoping to stand high in his lady's grace.
Embroidered was his clothing, like a bright
Field of fresh flowers, shining red and white.
Singing he was, or fluting, all the day—
He was as fresh as is the month of May.
Short was his gown; his sleeves were long and wide.
Well did he sit his horse, and nimbly ride;
He could make songs, intune them or indite;
Joust, play and dance, and also draw and write.
So well could he repeat love's endless tale,
He slept no more than does the nightingale.
Yet he was humble, courteous and able,
And carved before his father when at table.

A PRIORESS

There also was a nun, a Prioress
Whose smile was simple. Quiet, even coy,
The worst oath that she swore was, "By Saint Loy!"
And she was known as Sister Eglantine.
Sweetly she sang the services divine,
Intoning through her nose the melody.
Fairly she spoke her French, and skillfully,
After the style of Stratford-at-the-Bow—
Parisian French was not for her to know.
Precise at table and well-bred withal
Her lips would never let a morsel fall;
She never wet her fingers in her sauce,
But carried every tidbit without loss
Of even the smallest drop upon her breast.
Manners and good behavior pleased her best.
She always wiped her upper lip so clean
That not a speck of grease was ever seen
Upon the cup from which she drank. Her food
Was reached for neatly; she was never rude.

Though her demeanor was the very best,
Her mood was amiable, she loved a jest.
She always tried to copy each report
Of how the latest manner ran at court,
And yet to hold herself with dignity.
But, speaking of her inner nature, she
Was so devout, so full of sympathy,
She would lament if she would have to see
A mouse caught in a trap, or it had bled.
A few small dogs she had, and these she fed
With roasted meat, or milk and sweetened bread,
And wept aloud if one of them were dead,
Or if a person struck and made them smart—
She was all goodness and a tender heart.
Her wimple draped itself a modest way;
Her nose was straight, her eyes transparent grey,
Her mouth was small, but very soft and red,
Hers was a noble and a lovely head,
Almost a span in breadth, one realized;
For she was small but scarcely undersized.
Her cloak was well designed, you can be sure;
Her arm was graced with corals, and she wore
A string in which the green glass beads were bold,
And from it hung a brilliant brooch of gold
On which there was engraved a large, crowned *A*,
Followed by *Amor Vincit Omnia*.

A STUDENT

A Student came from Oxford town also,
Wedded to lore and logic long ago.
The horse he rode was lean as any rake;
Himself was scarcely fat, I'll undertake,
But spindling in his sad sobriety.
His overcoat was threadbare, too; for he
Was yet to win a single benefice,
And worldly thoughts of office were not his.
For he would rather have at his bed's head
Twenty great books, all bound in black or red,

Of Aristotle, his philosophy,
Than rich robes, fiddle, or gay psaltery.
Though a philosopher, he could not proffer
A treasury of gold from his scant coffer.
Anything he could borrow from a friend
On books and learning he would quickly spend,
And constantly he prayed for those who'd give
Help for the means by which his soul might live.
He gave most care to study and most heed;
Never a word he spoke beyond the need.
His speech was framed in form and reverence,
Pointed and quick and always packed with sense.
Moral his mind, and virtuous his speech;
And gladly would he learn, and gladly teach.

The tone of the tales varies with each speaker. It is both
merry and mocking in "The Nun's Priest's Tale," a half-humorous, half-moralizing variation of Aesop's fable about the sly
Raven and the foolish Fox. It is grim and bitter in "The
Pardoner's Tale," a masterpiece of suspense and horror. It is
naturally exciting in "The Knight's Tale," a romance of two
prisoner-knights and their love for the sister of their captor. It
is noble in "The Clerk's Tale," a story of Griselda, a model of
humility and patience whose goodness is finally rewarded. It is
triumphantly virtuous in "The Franklin's Tale," a dramatic
and uplifting story of two men in an impossible situation.

All the tales are told with startling directness. Sometimes
Chaucer mixes sentiment with solemnity, sometimes he adds a
moral. But more often than not, the story tells itself. Chaucer
rarely enters the tales; he lets them proceed with a minimum
of description and a maximum of talk, a conversation in which
the speakers remain true to themselves. Using the language of
his age, Chaucer, a great humorist as well as one of the greatest
of humanists, created a poetry which is ageless, a poetry which
has never been surpassed, if it has been equaled, for its vigor
and vitality.

At fifty Chaucer had been appointed Clerk of the King's

Works. In this position he was in charge of maintaining public buildings, parks, and repairs on Westminster Abbey. He had received various pensions, but living expenses had increased and the money was not enough to keep him out of debt. What is supposed to be his last poem was a disguised appeal to King Henry IV to aid him. One of the verses of his wry "Complaint to His Empty Purse" can be translated as follows:

> Vouchsafe this day (or it will be as night)
> That I the blissful sound of you may hear,
> Or see your color, like the sunlight bright,
> That for pure yellow never had a peer.
> You are my life; my wandering heart you steer.
> Queen of my comfort and good company,
> Once more be heavy, otherwise I die.

The sly appeal was heeded. The king doubled the poet's pension, and Chaucer, nearing sixty, signed a fifty-three-year lease for a house and garden near the great Gothic church he had helped to repair. Unfortunately, he did not live long to enjoy it. Less than a year after establishing himself in the new home, Chaucer became desperately ill—the plague was particularly violent in London at that time—and on October 25, 1400, he died. Honored with a tomb in Westminster Abbey, he was the first to be buried in the part which has become famous as the Poet's Corner.

Noble Gallant

SIR PHILIP SIDNEY
[1554–1586]

THE NAMES OF Sir Walter Raleigh and Sir Philip Sidney are usually paired. The similarities of the two men are striking, but so are their differences. They were born within two years of each other—Raleigh in 1552 and Sidney in 1554. Both were poets, gallants, soldiers, and court favorites who fell out of favor. However, Sidney was surrounded by friends, while Raleigh was hemmed in by enemies. Sidney was blessed with successes; Raleigh was doomed with failures. One met his death heroically on the battlefield; the other was charged with treason and beheaded. Raleigh wrote a few significant poems, but Sidney remains the more important poet.

Born November 30, 1554, at his father's luxurious estate in Pensonhurst, Kent, Sidney attended England's two leading universities, Oxford and Cambridge. Completing his education abroad, he traveled through France, Germany, and Italy. By the time he was twenty-two, he had captivated everyone at court. Queen Elizabeth made much of him; he was sent as her ambassador to princes and emperors in Europe. He returned in glory. A fellow poet, Fulke Greville, said he "carried grace and reverence above those of greater years. His very play tended to enrich his mind, so that even his teachers found something in him to observe and learn." Heir to the wealth of his uncle, the Earl of Leicester, he seemed sure of a golden future.

At a reception given for the queen at the home of Lord Essex, Sidney met and fell in love with Lord Essex's daughter, Penelope. She was eighteen, blonde, and beautiful. It appeared to be an excellent match; everyone doted on the lovely, modest girl and the brilliant young celebrity. There were rumors of an engagement. However, Penelope's father died and her mother remarried. Her mother's second husband was the Earl of Leicester; and, when she bore him a son, Sidney was no longer Leicester's heir. If there had been an engagement, it was broken, and Penelope was quickly married to a wealthy noble whose name was appropriately Lord Rich.

Sidney was heartbroken. Poetry saved him. "It is better to write," he said, "than lie and groan." Poem followed poem. Soon there were one hundred and eight sonnets, one hundred and eight declarations of his lost love, his memories of her tenderness, her touch and her kiss, his ecstasy and anguish. He slightly disguised the series by calling it *Astrophel and Stella.* But everyone knew that Stella was, literally, his star, and that Astrophel (meaning star-lover) was a Greek pun on Sidney's name; the old spelling was Astro*phil,* or Philip, lover of a star.

The series became enormously popular; it was responsible for a stream of sonnet sequences which followed. Sidney anticipated Shakespeare by being the first English poet to probe the rapture and the agony of love. Incidentally, the last line of the first sonnet might serve as a desk motto for any writer, young or old.

1

Loving in truth, and fain in verse my love to show,
That she, dear she, might take some pleasure of my pain,
Pleasure might cause her read, reading might make her know,
Knowledge might pity win, and pity grace obtain,
I sought fit words to paint the blackest face of woe,
Studying inventions fine, her wits to entertain,
Oft turning others' leaves, to see if thence would flow
Some fresh and fruitful showers upon my sunburnt brain.

But words came halting forth, wanting Invention's stay;
Invention, Nature's child, fled step-dame Study's blows;
And others' feet still seemed but strangers in my way.
Thus great with child to speak, and helpless in my throes,
Biting my truant pen, beating myself for spite:
"Fool!" said my Muse to me, "look in thy heart and write."

31

With how sad steps, O Moon, thou climb'st the skies,
How silently, and with how wan a face!
What, may it be that even in heav'nly place
That busy archer his sharp arrows tries?
Sure, if that long-with-love-acquainted eyes
Can judge of love, thou feel'st a lover's case.
I read it in thy looks: thy languisht grace,
To me, that feel the like, thy state decries.
Then, ev'n of fellowship, O Moon, tell me,
Is constant love deem'd there but want of wit?
Are beauties there as proud as here they be?
Do they above love to be lov'd, and yet
Those lovers scorn whom that love doth possess?
Do they call virtue there ungratefulness?

39

Come, Sleep! O Sleep, the certain knot of peace,
The baiting place of wit, the balm of woe,
The poor man's wealth, the prisoner's release,
Th' indifferent judge between the high and low;
With shield of proof shield me from out the prease[1]
Of those fierce darts Despair at me doth throw:
O, make in me those civil wars to cease;
I will good tribute pay if thou do so.
Take thou of me smooth pillows, sweetest bed,
A chamber deaf to noise and blind to light,
A rosy garland and a weary head:

[1] Press, multitude.

And if these things, as being thine in right,
Move not thy heavy grace, thou shalt in me
Livelier than elsewhere, Stella's image see.

54

Because I breathe not love to everyone,
Nor do not use set colors for to wear,
Nor nourish special locks of vowèd hair,
Nor give each speech a full point of a groan,
The courtly nymphs, acquainted with the moan
Of them who on their lips Love's standard bear,
"What, he!" say they of me. "Now I dare swear
He cannot love. No, no, let him alone."
And think so still, so Stella know my mind;
Profess indeed I do not Cupid's art;
But you, fair maids, at length this true shall find:
That his right badge is but worn in the heart.
Dumb swans, not chattering pies,[1] do lovers prove:
They love indeed who quake to say they love.

It is not known how long it took Sidney to recover from his
unhappiness, of if he recovered at all. In any case, he married
the daughter of Sir Frances Walsingham, and married well. He
sat in Parliament; he was knighted; he was appointed Governor
of Flushing. It is said that he refused the crown of Poland.

Sidney's birth had given him an auspicious beginning; his
death gave him an immortal end. In 1586 he went to the
Netherlands to fight for his country in its struggle with Spain.
At the battle of Zutphen he was badly wounded in the thigh.
As he was being carried off the field he called for water. At that
moment he saw a dying soldier staring at him. Sidney, turning
the flask aside, offered it to the poor man. "Drink," he said.
"Thy necessity is greater than mine." A few days later gangrene
set in, and he died October 17, 1586.

Sidney's place in literature was attained, apart from the son-

---

[1] Magpies.

nets, by his *Apology for Poetry*, afterward entitled *Defence of Poesie*, which is a spirited celebration rather than a defense. It marks the beginning of English literary criticism. "Nature never set forth the earth in so rich tapestry as poets have done," he wrote, "neither with pleasant rivers, fruitful trees, sweet smelling flowers, or whatever else may make the much loved earth more lovely." But his chief fame rests on the impassioned beauty of *Astrophel and Stella*—and one small lyric, one of the shortest, least artful, and most delightful of love songs.

> My true-love hath my heart, and I have his,
> By just exchange one for another given.
> I hold his dear, and mine he cannot miss,
> There never was a better bargain driven:
>   My true-love hath my heart, and I have his.
>
> His heart in me keeps him and me in one,
> My heart in him his thoughts and senses guides.
> He loves my heart, for once it was his own,
> I cherish his because in me it bides:
>   My true-love hath my heart, and I have his.

Eternal Lines

WILLIAM SHAKESPEARE
[1564–1616]

When in eternal lines to time thou grow'st,
So long as men can breathe or eyes can see,
So long lives this . . .

SHAKESPEARE was writing a sonnet about the power of love,
but he was also suggesting the power of poetry. No one ever
contributed more eternal lines to our literature—and to our
language—than Shakespeare. The *Oxford Dictionary of Quotations* devotes sixty-five double-column pages to quotable lines
from his works, more than twice as many pages as given to the
next most often quoted source, the Bible. We scarcely realize
how much of Shakespeare is put to use, how much of him has
become part of our everyday speech. Here are a few of his most
often quoted thoughts:

"All the world's a stage . . ." "Sermons in stones . . ."
"Thereby hangs a tale." (Those three are from *As You Like It.*)
"Neither a borrower nor a lender be . . ." "There are more
things in heaven and earth than are dreamt of in your philosophy . . ." "There is nothing good or bad, but thinking makes
it so . . ." "O! that this too, too solid flesh would melt . . ."
"To be or not to be; that is the question . . ." "The lady

37

doth protest too much . . ." "Sweets to the sweet . . ." "The rest is silence." (Those are from *Hamlet*.) "The better part of valor is discretion." (*King Henry IV, Part 1*.) "Uneasy lies the head that wears a crown." (*King Henry IV, Part 2*.) "What's mine is yours, and what's yours is mine." (*Measure for Measure*.) "It is a wise father that knows his own child . . ." "Love is blind, and lovers cannot see . . ." "The quality of mercy is not strained . . ." "How far that little candle throws his beams! So shines a good deed in a naughty world." (Those four are from *The Merchant of Venice*.) "If music be the food of love, play on . . ." "Some men are born great; some achieve greatness; and some have greatness thrust upon them." (*Twelfth Night*.) "Misery acquaints a man with strange bedfellows . . ." "O brave new world, that has such people in it!" (*The Tempest*.) "A horse! A horse! My kingdom for a horse!" (*King Richard III*.) "He jests at scars that never felt a wound . . ." "What's in a name? That which we call a rose, by any other name would smell as sweet . . ." "A plague on both your houses!" (*Romeo and Juliet*.) "The fault, dear Brutus, is not in our stars, but in ourselves . . ." "Cowards die many times before their deaths. The valiant never taste of death but once . . ." "I come to bury Caesar, not to praise him . . ." "This was the most unkindest cut of all." (*Julius Caesar*.)

And here are two famous contrasting passages from two other plays. The first occurs in the third act of *Othello* during a conversation between the villainous Iago and his too-trusting victim:

Who steals my purse, steals trash; 'tis something, nothing;
'Twas mine, 'tis his, and has been slave to thousands.
But he that filches from me my good name
Robs me of that which not enriches him,
And makes me poor indeed.

The second excerpt, from the last act of *Macbeth*, is Macbeth's despairing outburst when he hears of his wife's death and foresees his own doom:

Tomorrow, and tomorrow, and tomorrow,
Creeps in this petty pace from day to day,
To the last syllable of recorded time;
And all our yesterdays have lighted fools
The way to dusty death. Out, out, brief candle!
Life's but a walking shadow, a poor player
That struts and frets his hour upon the stage
And then is heard no more: it is a tale
Told by an idiot, full of sound and fury,
Signifying nothing.

William Shakespeare was born a little more than four hundred years ago, in late April. We are not sure of the exact day of his birth, but he was baptized on April 26, 1564. The place was a small town on a slowly winding river, Stratford-on-Avon. His mother was a farmer's daughter; his father was a leading citizen of the town, by profession a butcher, sometimes a glovemaker and a dealer in wool.

Sixteenth-century Stratford. was a prosperous as well as a lovely town. The gently rippling Avon wound between fields rich with oats, rye, wheat, and barley, and the legendary forest of Arden. The villagers lived well on all sorts of flesh, fish, and fowl. There were domestic hens and ducks, sheep for mutton, and beef cattle, as well as game—deer, hare, partridge, pigeons, wild geese—for the table, accompanied by various kinds of breads, puddings, and fruit. The food was washed down with cider, perry (made from pears), and ale. Except for the lordly mansions, houses were built of timber and thatched roofs; clay and loam filled up the spaces between the beams, which, exposed to the sun, turned a golden brown. Shakespeare may not have been reared in luxury, but he was brought up in comfort.

Although we have no authentic record of Shakespeare's education, it is almost certain that he attended the Stratford Grammar School, where, besides studying the Bible, geography and mathematics, he was taught not only Latin but also Latin literature. It seems that his retentive mind forgot nothing. He

relished and remembered the classic plays, the tragedies of
Seneca and the comedies of Terence—echoes from them are
heard in Shakespeare's dramas—but he cherished with equal
affection the popular songs of his day, the ballads sung and sold
on street corners and village greens. The ballads covered a
multitude of subjects—legends retold, heroic deeds renewed,
love stories, news of the moment, the current crime and the
latest rumor—all of them recounted in rhyme. It was only
natural that when Shakespeare began to write, he wrote in verse.
And it was natural that his audience listened to him without
effort, for the men and women of his time had been brought up
on poetry. Poetry was not a literary exercise but a common
language.

It is assumed that, after school hours, he helped his father,
carried messages for him, and waited on customers. He was little
more than a boy—eighteen—when he was married. His wife,
Anne Hathaway, a farmer's daughter from the neighboring village of Shottery, was eight years older than himself. Their first
child, Susanna, was christened six months later. Two other
children followed, twins named Hamnet and Judith.

Shakespeare did not remain long in Stratford. According to
one source, he ran away and served in the army when the
Spanish Armada threatened to invade England. Another tale
has it that he left home to become a country schoolteacher with
pupils scarcely younger than himself. A still more favorite story
tells how Shakespeare got into trouble when he joined a band
of young fellows who prowled through private preserves and
stole hare and venison. Poaching was a criminal offense, and
Shakespeare (so runs the story) was caught, whipped, and finally
driven out of the county. But these are legends. It is more likely
that he was fascinated by traveling players who toured the
countryside, fell in love with the lure of the stage, joined the
company, and went to London. This, too, is only a surmise.
But it has been definitely established that, by his mid-twenties,
Shakespeare was a member of the most important theatrical
company in England, an actor who was also a playwright.

William Davenant, a poet who used to boast that he was
Shakespeare's illegitimate son, claimed that he knew the facts.

According to Davenant, the stage-struck youth from Stratford was penniless and friendless when, following the troupe, he arrived in London. When he begged for work, he was told that there were no positions open except one: to guard the horses of the gentlemen who came to the theater. Shakespeare accepted and did so well at the task that he had to hire assistants, who became known as "Shakespeare's boys." He was also so affable that the actors found him a winning companion. Davenant says that he was "so acute and such a master of conversation that, struck therewith, they recommended him to the master of the house, in which he was first admitted in a low station." In other words, the manager was as much charmed as the actors and allowed Shakespeare to play small parts—Shakespeare's name appears in the cast of two of Ben Jonson's early plays. He was also permitted to revise and, to a great extent, rewrite other men's plays and even to collaborate with their authors. There was much competition in the theater; there was a constant demand for new plays or old plays brought up to date, and steady employment for those who could adapt them. It is probable that, besides making experiments of his own that have disappeared, Shakespeare was "mending" or "pointing" various plays before he was regarded as an outstanding dramatist.

We hear of his fame suddenly and in a curious way: through an attack by a rival poet, Robert Greene. Shakespeare was twenty-eight when Greene spitefully referred to him as "an upstart crow beautified with our feathers who supposes he can bombast out a blank verse as well as the best of you . . . an absolute *Johannes fac totum,* in his own conceit the only Shake-scene in the country." The *Johannes fac totum* is a sneering reference to a "Jack-of-all trades" who, still in his twenties, had startled his envious contemporaries by producing three historical plays about Henry the Sixth, at least one tragedy, and a couple of popular comedies. Greene's attack caused a controversy; Shakespeare was defended in public as well as in private. It was evident that he had made influential friends not only because of his work but by his quiet demeanor and dignity.

We can only guess at the way he looked. Shortly after his death a painted bust was erected above his grave, but it lacks expressiveness. It has been belittled as "a pudding-faced effigy" and "the portrait of a self-satisfied pork butcher," yet it is the only likeness we have which was made by a contemporary crafts-man who may have known Shakespeare, for his shop was near the theater. If the features are somewhat stolid, the forehead is high and noble—the modern poet Stephen Spender speaks of it as a "civilized dome riding all cities"—the hair is a reddish brown, and the eyes are speculative. In life the eyes must have brought animation to the face; they must have sparkled with merriment or burned with passion, for one of Shakespeare's fellow-poets speaks of him as a lively, handsome man.

Although he was a famous dramatist before he was thirty, the progress of Shakespeare's career as a playwright was tempo-rarily halted, for, from 1592 to 1594, the plague closed the theaters. During that interval he composed two erotic poems, "Venus and Adonis" and "The Rape of Lucrece." Both were dedicated to the young Earl of Southampton, a soldier, scholar, lover of the theater and, to judge from the warmth of the dedi-cations, a dear friend of the author. Shakespeare went to Ovid for the plots of both poems, but he altered the characterizations and added images which the Latin poet would have found strange. The first is by far the better poem. It is overdecorated, full of youthful excesses, but it has a quick-blooded, wild-hearted beauty. Coleridge said that in this narrative poem Shakespeare spoke as if he were a visitor from another planet, charmed and charming you "to gaze on the movements of Venus and Adonis as you would on the twinkling dances of vernal butterflies."

In his early thirties Shakespeare resumed the profession of playwriting. He was so well esteemed that Francis Meres, the sixteenth-century critic, rated him highest of all English drama-tists. Listing twelve of Shakespeare's plays, Meres wrote: "As Plautus and Seneca are accounted the best for comedy and tragedy among the Latins, so Shakespeare is the most excellent in both kinds for the stage." Then, speaking of the poems, Meres maintained that "the sweet and witty soul of Ovid lives in the mellifluous and honey-tongued Shakespeare."

It is also Meres who furnished a background to one of the greatest of the Shakespeare enigmas. Meres refers to Shakespeare's "sugared sonnets among his private friends." The sonnets were not published until Shakespeare was in his forties, but they were circulated among his "private friends" a dozen or more years before. Mystery continues to surround these one hundred and fifty-four poems. Part of the mystery is the dedication, which reads: "To the Onlie Begetter of these ensuing sonnets Mr. W. H. all happiness and that eternity promised by our ever-living poet wisheth the well-wishing adventurer in setting forth."

Nothing could be more ambiguous; countless battles have been fought over the phrase "onlie begetter" and the identity of "Mr. W. H." Some scholars believe that the publisher was thanking the holder of the manuscript (presumably "Mr. W. H.") for procuring the sonnets and allowing him to publish them. Since he got them, he was the "onlie begetter." However, the commonly accepted meaning is that "begetter" meant "inspirer," the person responsible for the creation of the poems, the one and only inspiration. Which brings us to the identity of "Mr. W. H."

Many candidates have been named for the honor, but most scholars believe that "W. H." is a disguised designation, a reversal of the initials H. W., or Henry Wriothesley, who was Shakespeare's patron and intimate friend, the Earl of Southampton. The sonnets themselves add plausibility to this assumption. They suggest a story concerning the poet, his love for a young nobleman, their rivalry for and separation by a woman, a "dark lady," and a delayed but final reconciliation. A clue is furnished by a sonnet which begins:

> Two loves I have of comfort and despair,
> Which, like two angels, do suggest me still:
> The better angel is a man right fair,
> The worser spirit a woman colored ill.

Although there is a drama of conflict running through the one hundred and fifty-four sonnets, the central theme is the strength of love. Subsidiary themes emphasize the idea of beauty, the swiftness of time, and the lasting power of poetry. Seldom have words achieved such verbal magic, such glorious images, such a variety of tone from the most delicate humor through the deepest passion to the most compelling nobility. "With this key," wrote Wordsworth, "Shakespeare unlocked his heart." The sonnets are unquestionably the most personal communications Shakespeare ever uttered. Free of the necessity of speaking through the characters in his plays, the poet is unreservedly himself. "Here," wrote the Danish critic George Brandes, "and here alone, we see Shakespeare himself, as distinct from his poetical creations—loving, admiring, longing, tortured, humiliated and adoring."

Every reader will make his own choice among the sonnets. Here, however, are ten eloquent examples which seem to be everyone's favorites.

18

Shall I compare thee to a summer's day?
Thou art more lovely and more temperate:
Rough winds do shake the darling buds of May,
And summer's lease hath all too short a date:
Sometimes too hot the eye of heaven shines,
And often is his gold complexion dimmed;
And every fair from fair sometime declines,
By chance, or nature's changing course untrimmed;
But thy eternal summer shall not fade,
Nor lose possession of that fair thou ow'st,
Nor shall Death brag thou wanderest in his shade,
When in eternal lines to time thou grow'st;
   So long as men can breathe, or eyes can see,
   So long lives this, and this gives life to thee.

19

Devouring Time, blunt thou the lion's paws,
And make the earth devour her own sweet brood;
Pluck the keen teeth from the fierce tiger's jaws,
And burn the long-lived phoenix in her blood;

Make glad and sorry seasons as thou fleet'st,
And do whate'er thou wilt, swift-footed Time,
To the wide world and all her fading sweets.
But I forbid thee one most heinous crime:
O, carve not with thy hours my love's fair brow,
Nor draw no lines there with thine antique pen;
Him in thy course untainted do allow
For beauty's pattern to succeeding men.
    Yet do thy worst, old Time: despite thy wrong,
    My love shall in my verse ever live young.

29

When in disgrace with fortune and men's eyes
I all alone beweep my outcast state,
And trouble deaf heaven with my bootless cries,
And look upon myself and curse my fate,
Wishing me like to one more rich in hope,
Featured like him, like him with friends possessed,
Desiring this man's art, and that man's scope,
With what I most enjoy contented least.
Yet in these thoughts myself almost despising,
Haply I think on thee—and then my state,
Like to the lark at break of day arising
From sullen earth, sings hymns at heaven's gate;
    For thy sweet love remembered, such wealth brings
    That then I scorn to change my state with kings.

30

When to the sessions of sweet silent thought
I summon up remembrance of things past,
I sigh the lack of many a thing I sought,
And with old woes new wail my dear time's waste:
Then can I drown an eye, unused to flow,
For precious friends hid in death's dateless night,
And weep afresh love's long since cancelled woe,
And moan the expense of many a vanished sight:

Then can I grieve at grievances foregone,
And heavily from woe to woe tell o'er
The sad account of fore-bemoanèd moan,
Which I new pay as if not paid before.
    But if the while I think on thee, dear friend,
    All losses are restored and sorrows end.

33

Full many a glorious morning have I seen
Flatter the mountain-tops with sovereign eye,
Kissing with golden face the meadows green,
Gilding pale streams with heavenly alchemy;
Anon permit the basest clouds to ride
With ugly rack on his celestial face,
And from the forlorn world his visage hide,
Stealing unseen to west with this disgrace:
Even so my sun one early morn did shine,
With all-triumphant splendor on my brow;
But out! alack! he was but one hour mine,
The region cloud hath masked him from me now.
    Yet him for this my love no whit disdaineth;
    Suns of the world may stain when heaven's sun staineth.

73

That time of year thou may'st in me behold
When yellow leaves, or none, or few, do hang
Upon these boughs which shake against the cold,
Bare ruined choirs, where late the sweet birds sang.
In me thou seest the twilight of such day
As after sunset fadeth in the west,
Which, by and by, black night doth take away.
Death's second self, that seals up all in rest:
In me thou seest the glowing of such fire
That on the ashes of his youth doth lie,
As the death-bed whereon it must expire,
Consumed with that which it was nourished by.
    This thou perceiv'st, which makes thy love more strong,
    To love that well which thou must leave ere long.

87

Farewell! thou art too dear for my possessing,
And like enough thou know'st thy estimate:
The charter of thy worth gives thee releasing;
My bonds in thee are all determinate.
For how do I hold thee but by thy granting?
And for that riches where is my deserving?
The cause of this fair gift in me is wanting,
And so my patent back again is swerving.
Thyself thou gav'st, thy own worth then not knowing,
Or me, to whom thou gav'st it, else mistaking;
So thy great gift, upon misprision[1] growing,
Comes home again, on better judgment making.
    Thus have I had thee, as a dream doth flatter,
    In sleep, a king; but waking, no such matter.

94

They that have power to hurt, and will do none,
That do not do the thing they most do show,
Who, moving others, are themselves as stone,
Unmoved, cold, and to temptation slow—
They rightly do inherit heaven's graces,
And husband nature's riches from expense;
They are the lords and owners of their faces,
Others, but stewards of their excellence.
The summer's flower is to the summer sweet
Though to itself it only live and die,
But if that flower with base infection meet,
The basest weed outbraves his dignity:
    For sweetest things turn sourest by their deeds;
    Lilies that fester smell far worse than weeds.

106

When in the chronicle of wasted time
I see descriptions of the fairest wights,[2]
And beauty making beautiful old rhyme
In praise of ladies dead, and lovely knights,

[1] Mistake.   [2] Persons.

Then, in the blazon of sweet beauty's best,
Of hand, of foot, of lip, of eye, of brow,
I see their antique pen would have expressed
Even such a beauty as you master now.
So all their praises are but prophecies
Of this our time, all you prefiguring;
And, for they looked but with divining eyes,
They had not skill enough your worth to sing!
   For we, which now behold these present days,
   Have eyes to wonder, but lack tongues to praise.

116

Let me not to the marriage of true minds
Admit impediments. Love is not love
Which alters when it alteration finds,
Or bends with the remover to remove.
O no! it is an ever-fixèd mark
That looks on tempests, and is never shaken;
It is the star to every wandering bark,
Whose worth's unknown, although his height be taken.
Love's not Time's fool, though rosy lips and cheeks
Within his bending sickle's compass come;
Love alters not with his brief hours and weeks,
But bears it out even to the edge of doom.
   If this be error and upon me proved,
   I never writ, nor no man ever loved.

Shakespeare was as successful financially as he was creatively, but his pleasure in success was marred by the death of his son Hamnet. He returned to Stratford for the funeral and began making plans for retirement there. He had become part owner of the newly built and prospering Globe theater, and his financial rewards were such that he was able to buy New Place, one of the finest houses in his native town, purchase more than a hundred acres of good land for farming, and not only pay his father's debts but also obtain for him a coat of arms so that his father could not be considered a mere tradesman. But, although he longed for the quiet of the country around Stratford, for twenty years Shakespeare continued to write and revise the plays which were bringing him an accumulating fortune. Until he was almost fifty, his life was the London theater. After the panoply of the historical plays and the lyric romanticism of *Romeo and Juliet,* comedy became his favorite medium. His fondness for the comic spirit infiltrates his most serious dramas and laughs its way, sometimes gently, sometimes riotously, through *As You Like It, The Taming of the Shrew, The Comedy of Errors, A Midsummer Night's Dream, Twelfth Night,* and *Much Ado About Nothing.*

With the approach of middle age Shakespeare grew more somber; careless delight gave way to disillusion and darkness. This period is marked by four great tragedies surpassing in depth and penetration anything he had previously attempted. All four are profound revelations of human distress. *Hamlet* vibrates with the tensions of an agonized spirit torn between action and meditation, a play which, incidentally, is so much a part of our inheritance that it seems to be constructed of familiar quotations. *Othello* is a heartbreaking exhibit of deception, of unscrupulous villainy and self-destructive jealousy. *Macbeth* is a study of hideous ambition, a lust for power which forces a weak man and a masterful woman to become murderers. *King Lear* is an almost unbearable struggle between good and evil, of blind innocence and insane passion. The so-called Roman plays—*Julius Caesar, Antony and Cleopatra,* and *Coriolanus*—also belong to this period, followed by the Greek plays: *Troilus and Cressida* and *Timon of Athens.*

In his final phase Shakespeare rose above despair. He grew more tolerant of humanity's failings; he explored the emotions with new sympathy and wisdom. His genius is revealed equally in the charm of *A Winter's Tale* and in the magnificence of *The Tempest.* Presumably Shakespeare's valedictory work, *The Tempest* identifies the creator with his creation. Prospero's abnegation sounds like Shakespeare's resignation, his farewell to the stage:

> Our revels now are ended. These our actors,
> As I foretold you, were all spirits, and
> Are melted into air, into thin air:
> And, like the baseless fabric of this vision,
> The cloud-capped towers, the gorgeous palaces,
> The solemn temples, the great globe itself,
> Yea, all which it inherit, shall dissolve,
> And, like this insubstantial pageant faded,
> Leave not a rack behind. We are such stuff
> As dreams are made on, and our little life
> Is rounded with a sleep.

Like Chaucer, Shakespeare invented few plots of his own. He took his story line from every conceivable source, from scripts by his contemporaries and from such ancients as Plutarch and Ovid, from the tales of Boccaccio and the accounts of Holinshed, whose *Chronicles of England, Scotland, and Ireland* contained the germs of Shakespeare's historical plays. He wrote in a restless energy of creativity and in every vein. Yet he was not sorry to abandon his work at the height of his fame. "This rough magic I here abjure" is what Prospero the enchanter says toward the end of *The Tempest,* but there is little doubt that it is Shakespeare's voice speaking. "I'll break my staff—I'll drown my book." In the prime of life Shakespeare figuratively broke his magic staff, drowned his book, left everything that London could offer, and retired to New Place in rural Stratford.

He was not lonely. His daughter Judith was the wife of a neighbor; his elder daughter, Susanna, was married to Doctor Hall, the most renowned physician in the district. He had visitors from the city, entertained old friends, and made new ones. It is presumed that he had suffered from the strain of writing the great tragedies, that he may have had a breakdown in his fiftieth year. We cannot be sure of this. However, we know that he foresaw his end. He made a will providing for old associates as well as relatives, even for unborn grandchildren. A few weeks after signing the will he died, ironically enough on the probable day of his birth, April 23, 1616. He was fifty-two years old.

Even had Shakespeare not written some of the greatest dramas ever conceived, he would still be acclaimed one of the world's greatest poets. Besides the imperishable sonnets, his reputation could rest on the songs which intersperse the plays. Some of the loveliest lyrics in the language were composed not for their own sake but as theatrical devices. They were meant to emphasize a situation, relieve a crisis, prepare an entrance, or bring a scene to a close. The lyrics were sung, not recited; the printed page cannot give them full effect. Shakespeare lived in a golden age of music. Many Elizabethan poets were also composers; Shakespeare continually pays tribute to music's persuasion. He speaks of "Music with her silver sounds" and "If music be the food of love, play on," and

> The man that hath no music in himself,
> Nor is not moved with concord of sweet sounds,
> Is fit for treasons, strategems, and spoils.

Love's Labor's Lost ends with a pair of matched songs. The first is sung by Ver (Spring) clothed in the feathers of the vernal cuckoo; the second is sung by Hiems (Winter) dressed like a snow owl. The first, incidentally, discloses Shakespeare's fondness for punning; the word "cuckoo" is mockingly "unpleasing to the married ear" because it sounds like "cuckold," a deceived husband. Winter itself is felt in the second song with Tom carrying in the logs under the icicles, Dick trying to warm his freezing fingers, Marian's red nose, and Joan stirring her pot in the steaming kitchen, while roasted crab apples add spice to a bowl of hot wine.

1

> When daisies pied and violets blue,
>   And lady-smocks all silver-white,
> And cuckoo-buds of yellow hue
>   Do paint the meadows with delight,
> The cuckoo then, on every tree,
> Mocks married men, for thus sings he:
> "Cuckoo! cuckoo!" O word of fear,
> Unpleasing to a married ear.

When shepherds pipe on oaten straws,
    And merry larks are ploughmen's clocks,
When turtles tread, and rooks, and daws,
    And maidens bleach their summer smocks,
The cuckoo then, on every tree,
Mocks married men, for thus sings he:
"Cuckoo! cuckoo!" O word of fear,
Unpleasing to a married ear.

2

When icicles hang by the wall
    And Dick the shepherd blows his nail,
And Tom bears logs into the hall,
    And milk comes frozen home in pail;
When blood is nipped, and ways be foul,
Then nightly sings the staring owl
"To-whit! Tu-whoo!" A merry note,
While greasy Joan doth keel the pot.

When all aloud the wind doth blow,
    And coughing drowns the parson's saw,
And birds sit brooding in the snow,
    And Marian's nose looks red and raw;
When roasted crabs hiss in the bowl—
Then nightly sings the staring owl
"To-whit! Tu-whoo!" A merry note,
While greasy Joan doth keel the pot.

As You Like It is a pastoral comedy in which it is said Shakespeare played one of the characters. Much of the action takes place in the forest of Arden, and the setting is made more colorful by the introduction of songs about the greenwood. Here are three that almost make their own music.

1

Under the greenwood tree
    Who loves to lie with me,
    And turn his merry note
    Unto the sweet bird's throat,

Come hither, come hither, come hither:
  Here shall he see
  No enemy
But winter and rough weather.

Who doth ambition shun,
  And loves to live i' the sun,
  Seeking the food he eats,
  And pleased with what he gets,
Come hither, come hither, come hither:
  Here shall he see
  No enemy
But winter and rough weather.

2

  Blow, blow, thou winter wind,
  Thou art not so unkind
    As man's ingratitude;
  Thy tooth is not so keen,
  Because thou art not seen,
    Although thy breath be rude.
Heigh-ho! sing, heigh-ho! unto the green holly:
Most friendship is feigning, most loving mere folly.
    Then heigh-ho! the holly!
    This life is most jolly.

  Freeze, freeze, thou bitter sky,
  That dost not bite so nigh
    As benefits forgot:
  Though thou the waters warp,
  Thy sting is not so sharp
    As friend remembered not.
Heigh-ho! sing, heigh-ho! unto the green holly:
Most friendship is feigning, most loving mere folly.
    Then heigh-ho! the holly!
    This life is most jolly.

3

It was a lover and his lass,
　With a hey, and a ho, and a hey nonino,
That o'er the green corn-field did pass
　In the spring-time, the only pretty ring-time,
When birds do sing, hey ding a ding, ding!
　Sweet lovers love the spring.

Between the acres of the rye,
　With a hey, and a ho, and a hey nonino,
These pretty country folks would lie,
　In spring-time, the only pretty ring-time,
When birds do sing, hey ding a ding, ding!
　Sweet lovers love the spring.

This carol they began that hour,
　With a hey, and a ho, and a hey nonino,
How that a life was but a flower
　In spring-time, the only pretty ring-time,
When birds do sing, hey ding a ding, ding!
　Sweet lovers love the spring.

And therefore take the present time,
　With a hey, and a ho, and a hey nonino,
For love is crownèd with the prime
　In spring-time, the only pretty ring-time,
When birds do sing, hey ding a ding, ding!
　Sweet lovers love the spring.

Perhaps the three most famous of Shakespeare's songs—those which have been set to music most often by composers from the sixteenth-century Thomas Morley to the nineteenth-century Franz Schubert—are not from his most important plays. They are "Who is Silvia?" from *Two Gentlemen of Verona*, "Hark! hark! the lark" from *Cymbeline*, and "O mistress mine" from *Twelfth Night*. Seldom have words been distilled into such perfect sounds.

1

Who is Silvia? What is she,
   That all our swains commend her?
Holy, fair, and wise is she;
   The heaven such grace did lend her,
That she might admirèd be.

Is she kind as she is fair?
   For beauty lives with kindness.
Love doth to her eyes repair,
   To help him of his blindness;
And, being helped, inhabits there.

Then to Silvia let us sing,
   That Silvia is excelling;
She excels each mortal thing,
   Upon the dull earth dwelling:
To her let us garlands bring.

2

Hark! hark! the lark at heaven's gate sings,
   And Phoebus 'gins arise,
His steeds to water at those springs
   On chaliced flowers that lies;
And winking mary-buds begin
   To ope their golden eyes.
With every thing that pretty is,
   My lady sweet, arise;
      Arise, arise!

3

O mistress mine, where are you roaming?
O stay and hear, your true love's coming,
   That can sing both high and low.
Trip no further, pretty sweeting;
Journeys end in lovers' meeting,
   Every wise man's son doth know.

What is love? 'tis not hereafter;
Present mirth hath present laughter;
What's to come is still unsure:
In delay there lies no plenty—
Then come kiss me, sweet-and-twenty,
Youth's a stuff will not endure.

For Shakespeare, the world's superlative writer, no superlatives are too excessive. He probed every aspect of humanity; he expressed all the pleasures which delight men as well as the passions which destroy them. In his magnificent reflectiveness he was the mirror of mankind. Coleridge called him "myriad-minded"; countless other admirers have echoed Ben Jonson, who loved the man and honored his memory "on this side idolatry." His range is immeasurable, his understanding is illimitable, and his appeal is always as timely as it is timeless.

"No Man Is an Island"

JOHN DONNE
[1572–1631]

THE POETRY OF John Donne is a supreme example of the physical joined to the metaphysical. What is physical needs no further explanation; the metaphysical is less easy to define. In an introduction to *Metaphysical Lyrics and Poems of the Seventeenth Century*, Sir Herbert Grierson wrote that metaphysical poetry "is a poetry which has been inspired by a philosophical conception of the universe and the role suggested to the human spirit in the great drama of existence." Therefore, the metaphysical poet is one whose imagination is intensified to such a degree that the expression of his spiritual life becomes the drama of human life itself.

More than any other poet except Shakespeare, Donne united thought and feeling, sense and sensibility. Son of a prosperous merchant, descended on his mother's side from the great humanist Sir Thomas More, he was born in London in 1572. His life was a long struggle between flesh and spirit, between the body (which he regarded as his everyday "book") and the soul, the final mystery. A precocious child, he entered Oxford at twelve and Cambridge at fifteen. At eighteen he returned to London, studied law, was admitted to the bar, although he did not practice the profession, became involved in controversies between

57

Catholics and Protestants, and abandoned his forefather's Catholic faith to join the Church of England.

He was still a youth when he inherited a fortune and proceeded to enjoy it. He loved travel, lived lightly and wrote lighthearted, lusty, and sometimes cynical songs and satires. Though none of these was printed, they were circulated privately and were much sought after. One of the lightest, an amusing reproof to "The Sun Rising," begins:

> Busy old fool, unruly Sun,
>   Why dost thou thus,
> Through windows, and through curtains, call on us?
> Must to thy motions lovers' seasons run?
>   Saucy pedantic wretch, go chide
>   Late school-boys and sour prentices,
>   Go tell court-huntsmen that the king will ride,
>   Call country ants to harvest offices.
> Love, all alike, no season knows nor clime,
> Nor hours, days, months, which are the rags of time.

In his mid-twenties Donne saw service with the earl of Essex, sailed on hazardous expeditions, and took part in the victory of the warship appropriately named "Repulse." Back in England he became secretary to Sir Thomas Egerton, the eminent Lord Keeper of the Great Seal.

The enviable appointment had consequences which, instead of advancing his career, almost ruined him. Tall, handsome, gracious as well as graceful, Donne had always been pursued by women; he had been in and out of love several times before he met and was fascinated by young Anne More. She idolized him. Anne was Lady Egerton's sixteen-year-old niece, and Donne, at twenty-eight, fell recklessly in love with her. Fearing that he never would get permission to marry his beloved, he persuaded her to elope with him and the two were married secretly. A marriage without the consent of the family was considered as bad as an abduction, and Lord Egerton not only dismissed Donne from his service but had him thrown into prison. It was several weeks before he was released, and a year before the clandestine marriage was legalized.

Meanwhile, Donne's situation had become desperate. He summed it up in an unhappy pun: "John Donne—Anne Donne —Undone!" Although there was a kind of reconciliation, the young couple had to struggle to maintain their household. Donne had squandered his inheritance during his days of travel and careless living; he had no position that yielded a steady income; children arrived and had to be cared for, clothed, and fed. Lord Egerton helped a little from time to time, but Donne and his wife lived like poor people. Chances of a court career had vanished; no one offered him even a scanty livelihood. Defeated and depressed, he confessed himself a failure. "Methinks I have the keys of my prison in my own hand, and no remedy presents itself so soon to my heart as mine own sword." For thirteen years he fought against the "sickly inclination" of suicide.

It was not until Donne was past forty that the unhappy period ended. King James I gave him a firm position in the Church and, seven years later, Donne, at forty-eight, was promoted to the high rank of Dean of St. Paul's. It seemed as if, at last, his troubles were over. But, two years later, his beloved wife, still in her thirties, died in childbirth. She had borne him many children; the strain was too much for her. Donne was devastated. Sunk in sorrow and racked with remorse, he felt he had dragged Anne down from a life of ease to poverty and death. He turned abruptly away from every form of pleasure and gave himself desperately to preaching.

As a young man Donne delighted in the composition of love poems. Two of the most admired were the intense and introspective "The Good Morrow" and the simple but impassioned "Break of Day."

THE GOOD MORROW

I wonder, by my troth, what thou and I
Did, till we loved? Were we not weaned till then?
But sucked on country pleasures, childishly?
Or snorted we in the Seven Sleepers' den?

'Twas so; but this, all pleasures fancies be;
If ever any beauty I did see,
Which I desired, and got, 'twas but a dream of thee.

And now good morrow to our waking souls,
Which watch not one another out of fear;
For love all love of other sights controls,
And makes one little room an everywhere.
Let sea-discoverers to new worlds have gone;
Let maps to other, worlds on worlds have shown;
Let us possess one world; each hath one, and is one.

My face in thine eye, thine in mine appears,
And true plain hearts do in the faces rest;
Where can we find two better hemispheres
Without sharp north, without declining west?
Whatever dies, was not mix'd equally.
If our two loves be one, or thou and I
Love so alike that none can slacken, none can die.

BREAK OF DAY

Stay, O sweet, and do not rise.
The light that shines comes from thine eyes;
The day breaks not; it is my heart,
Because that you and I must part.
    Stay—or else my joys will die
    And perish in their infancy.

After Anne's death Donne put all his energies into sermons
and transformed his sufferings into religious poems. In his
appreciative biography of Donne, Izaak Walton, the English
author famous for *The Compleat Angler,* wrote that at this time
"grief took so full possession of his heart as to leave no place
for joy. . . . He bemoaned himself without restraint." Religion
became his refuge. Donne's *Divine Poems* are full of tension,
even violence, but they were his release. His poems took an
entirely new direction. They continued to be full of elaborate
and often fantastic images, but they reached a dignity, a high

austerity, that his previous poems had never attained. One of the "Holy Sonnets" is not only a repudiation of suicidal thoughts but also a refusal to fear the threat of death.

> Death, be not proud, though some have callèd thee
> Mighty and dreadful, for thou art not so;
> For those whom thou think'st thou dost overthrow
> Die not, poor Death; nor yet canst thou kill me.
> From rest and sleep, which but thy picture be,
> Much pleasure. Then from thee much more must flow;
> And soonest our best men with thee do go—
> Rest of their bones and souls' delivery!
>
> Thou'rt slave to fate, chance, kings, and desperate men,
> And dost with poison, war, and sickness dwell;
> And poppy or charms can make us sleep as well
> And better than thy stroke. Why swell'st thou then?
> One short sleep past, we wake eternally,
> And Death shall be no more. Death, thou shalt die.

Another of the sonnets confesses Donne's great need of God. It is a strange confession. In a long and involved figure of speech, the poet compares himself to a walled city that longs to open its gates to the conqueror but cannot surrender until it is completely assaulted and captured. The town—the soul—must be seized by the conqueror: God.

> Batter my heart, three-personed God; for you
> As yet but knock, breathe, shine, and seek to mend.
> That I may rise and stand, o'erthrow me and bend
> Your force to break, blow, burn, and make me new.
> I, like an usurped town, to another due.
> Labor to admit you, but, oh, to no end;
> Reason, your viceroy in me, me should defend,
> But is captived and proves weak or untrue.
>
> Yet dearly I love you and would be loved fain,
> But am betrothed unto your enemy:
> Divorce me, untie or break that knot again,
> Take me to you, imprison me, for I,

Except you enthrall me, never shall be free,
Nor ever chaste, except you ravish me.

Donne became the most famous preacher of his day. His
sermons were fiery and rich in rhetoric. His listeners felt they
were magnificent performances and almost applauded at the end
of what often sounded like operatic arias. He preached with
such force and fervor that his health failed. He began to medi-
tate much on man's mortality. He posed for a funeral statue
which was set up in St. Paul's. He had himself painted in a
shroud, his eyes shut, his lips closed, with just enough of the
sheet turned back to show a thin, pale face. He kept the portrait
by his bedside, "his hourly object until his death." When he
died, March 12, 1631, he was survived by six children and a
few poems. While he was alive only two poems had been published; the rest had been passed from hand to hand. The first
edition of his work—a memorable collection—was not published until some time after his death.

A few years later Donne fell out of favor; the next generation
considered him scarcely worthy of notice. The eighteenth century scorned him. That formidable critic Samuel Johnson con-
ceded that the metaphysical poets were men of learning but, he
added wryly, "learning was their whole endeavor. Instead of
writing poetry they only wrote verses . . . and the modulation
was so imperfect that they were found to be verses only by
counting the syllables." As late as its 1940 edition, the *Encyclo-
pedia Britannica* was maintaining in an article by Edmund
Gosse that though "the influence of Donne upon the literature
of England was singularly wide and deep, it was almost wholly
malign."

It was not until the middle of the twentieth century that the
more sensitive poets and critics "discovered" Donne. They recognized that his troubled, introspective spirit was the spirit of
their own times, and that Donne's conflict between hope and
disillusion was as characteristic of our age as it was of his. Three
centuries after his death, one of the most impassioned of modern
novels, Ernest Hemingway's *For Whom the Bell Tolls,* owed

its title as well as its underlying idea to a few lines in one of Donne's "Devotions." These are the unforgettable lines:

"No man is an island, entire of itself. Every man is a piece of the continent, a part of the main. If a clod be washed away by the sea, Europe is the less, as well as if a promontory were, as well as if a manor of thy friends or thine own were. Any man's death diminishes me, because I am involved in mankind. And, therefore, never send to know for whom the bell tolls. It tolls for thee."

"Brooks, Blossoms, Birds, and Bowers"

ROBERT HERRICK
[1591–1674]

IT WOULD BE hard to imagine a greater contrast than the poetry
of John Donne and the poetry of Robert Herrick. The men
themselves had many similarities. They were born in London
within a few miles and a few years of each other. Both took
holy orders. Both preached to sometimes bored and sometimes
bewildered congregations. Both composed light verses as well
as pious epistles. Both wrote many variations on the theme of
human love.

The contrasts, however, are in every line they wrote, in their
very manner of writing. To Donne most things evoked either
anxiety or agony. To Herrick everything was a delight; even
his occasional protest is little more than a pout. Donne assaults
the reader with fierce intensity; Herrick coaxes the reader with
continual playfulness. It is too much of a simplification to say
that Herrick took life lightly and Donne saw it "through a
glass, darkly," but there is some truth in the statement. Rarely
have there been two poets with so many thoughts in common
but so opposed in style and treatment.

Baptized on August 24, 1591, Robert Herrick had been born
into a family of jewelers. Both his father and his uncle were
among the richest goldsmiths of the day, and it is not too fanciful

to believe that Herrick brought the jeweler's fine craftsmanship into the making of his delicately wrought stanzas. There were seven children, and when the father died shortly after the birth of Robert, his seventh, the uncle brought them up.

For ten years the boy was apprenticed to his uncle, but William Herrick saw things in the growing youth that made him determine not to allow Robert to follow the family trade but to have him educated at one of the great colleges. Accordingly Robert was sent to Cambridge, where he received his B.A. in his twenty-sixth year. Two years later he became Master of Arts, and, having studied for the ministry, he was ordained at thirty-two.

Nothing is known of his next six years. However, it is evident from poems written during this period that Herrick must have moved in a literary circle. He was not only popular but so well-liked that he became the protégé of Ben Jonson and, in return, wrote several charming verses to that famous Elizabethan poet and playwright. When Herrick was thirty-eight he obtained what seemed to be a promising position: a "living" presented to him by King Charles I. It was the vicarage of Dean Prior in Devonshire. There he spent eighteen years of his life. The countryside was lovely. Nature brought out the pagan as well as the poet in him. In a rhymed foreword to his poems he said:

> I sing of brooks, of blossoms, birds, and bowers,
> Of April, May, of June, and July flowers . . .
> I write of youth and love, and have access
> By these, to sing of cleanly wantonness . . .
> I sing of times trans-shifting, and I write
> How roses first came red and lilies white.

Herrick should have been happy in Dean Prior. But the village was remote, there was no intellectual stimulation, the inhabitants were dull. Aware of Herrick's discontent, the villagers resented him, and he, in turn, offended them. It is said that once, annoyed by the inattention of his listeners, he cursed the members of his congregation and threw the pages of his sermon at them. He pictured his neighbors as:

> A people currish, churlish as the seas;
> And rude, almost, as rudest savages.

He missed his beloved London; he felt bitterly isolated. He complained:

> London my home is, though by hard fate sent
> Into a long and dreary banishment.

Having supported the king during the Civil War, he was no longer favored by the government when the Puritans came to power. He lost his position in the Kentish village and was glad to return to London. "I fly to thee," he wrote, "blest place of my nativity." He resolved to re-establish himself among his fellow-poets and published everything he had written, considerably more than a thousand poems, in a volume entitled *Hesperides*. It was a failure. The vogue of Ben Jonson and the Elizabethans was over. The taste now was for Donne and the intellectual, highly sophisticated wits. Herrick was considered old-fashioned. His contemporaries belittled him and the next generation ignored him. More than a century passed before Herrick's unpretentious charm was acknowledged.

After the monarchy had been restored, Herrick's pulpit was given back to him. He was old now—seventy-one—and he enjoyed his life in rural Devonshire. He spent the last twelve years of his life there and died October 15, 1674, two months after his eighty-third birthday.

A country clergyman, Herrick composed many religious poems—he called them "Noble Numbers"—but he was most himself when he wrote of "brooks, of blossoms, birds, and bowers," and the lush, lawless beauty of the pastoral scene. He never married, yet his love poems are among the liveliest, most romantic lyrics in literature. They retain their freshness and delicacy. Herrick's book presents a parade of ladies who may or may not have been real, but their very names—Corinna, Anthea, Electra, Biancha, Myrrha, Perenna, Flora, Silvia, and, most of all, Julia—leave a trail of exquisite perfume through the lines. It was Julia who inspired fifty poems of worship. The following is one of the most famous: "Night-Piece to Julia."

Her eyes the glow-worm lend thee;
The shooting stars attend thee;
   And the elves also.
   Whose little eyes glow
Like the sparks of fire, befriend thee.

No will-o'-the-wisp mis-light thee;
Nor snake, or slow-worm bite thee;
   But on, on thy way,
   Not making a stay,
Since ghost there's none to affright thee.

Let not the dark thee cumber;
What though the moon does slumber?
   The stars of the night
   Will lend thee their light,
Like tapers clear without number.

Then, Julia, let me woo thee,
Thus, thus to come unto me;
   And when I shall meet
   Thy silv'ry feet,
My soul I'll pour into thee.

Even lovelier is the tiny "Upon Julia's Clothes." Here, in six brief lines, is one of the silkiest poems ever written. The syllables themselves, with their sliding *l's* and silky *s's,* suggest the rustling texture, the flowing "liquefaction" and shining "vibration" of the beloved's garments.

Whenas in silks my Julia goes
Then, then (methinks) how sweetly flows
That liquefaction of her clothes.

Next, when I cast mine eyes and see
That brave vibration each way free;
O how that glittering taketh me!

Herrick liked his ladies to be seen at their best. He echoed Ben Jonson:

Still to be neat, still to be drest,
As you were going to a feast.

But he did not insist on a taste that was too finicky. He claimed that sometimes a "small neglect," with loose robes and hair flowing free, was entrancing. He made it plain in his "Delight in Disorder."

> A sweet disorder in the dress
> Kindles in clothes a wantonness:
> A lawn about the shoulders thrown
> Into a fine distractión,
> An erring lace, which here and there
> Enthralls the crimson stomacher,
> A cuff neglectful, and thereby
> Ribbands to flow confusedly,
> A winning wave (deserving note)
> In the tempestuous petticoat,
> A careless shoe-string, in whose tie
> I see a wild civility,
> Do more bewitch me, than when art
> Is too precise in every part.

Perhaps the most characteristic as well as the most anthologized of Herrick's poems, "To the Virgins To Make Much of Time," is a universal reflection. It says what it has to say as clearly to the twentieth century as it did to the seventeenth.

> Gather ye rose-buds while ye may,
>   Old Time is still a-flying:
> And this same flower that smiles today,
>   Tomorrow will be dying.
>
> The glorious lamp of heaven, the Sun,
>   The higher he's a-getting
> The sooner will his race be run,
>   And nearer he's to setting.
>
> That age is best which is the first,
>   When youth and blood are warmer;
> But being spent, the worse, and worst
>   Times, still succeed the former.

Then be not coy, but use your time;
   And while ye may, go marry:
For having lost but once your prime,
   You may for every tarry.

No picture of Herrick would be complete without at least a
token representation of his flower pieces. Here are two of the
tenderest ("To Daffodils" and "To Daisies"), and the second
turns out to be another love poem to Julia.

Fair daffodils, we weep to see
   You haste away so soon;
As yet the early-rising sun
   Has not attained his noon.
      Stay, stay,
    Until the hasting day
      Has run
   But to the even-song;
And, having prayed together, we
   Will go with you along.

We have short time to stay, as you;
   We have as short a spring;
As quick a growth to meet decay,
   As you, or any thing.
      We die,
   As your hours do, and dry
      Away
   Like to the summer's rain;
Or as the pearls of morning's dew,
   Ne'er to be found again.

*

Shut not so soon; the dull-eyed night
   Has not as yet begun
To make a seizure on the light,
   Or to seal up the sun.

No marigolds yet closèd are:
　No shadows great appear;
Nor doth the early shepherd's star
　Shine like a spangle here.

Stay but till my Julia close
　Her life-begetting eye;
And let the whole world then dispose
　Itself to live or die.

Herrick was not always sweet and airy. He had his grim
moments. But even his grimness has a dainty touch and a gay
undertone. "The Hag," for example, is about a witch, yet the
picture presented will frighten no one. The tripping little
rhymes are too light for fearfulness, and the terror produced
is only a mock horror.

The hag is astride
This night for to ride,
The devil and she together;
　Through thick and through thin,
　Now out and then in,
Though ne'er so foul be the weather.

A thorn or a burr
She takes for a spur;
With a lash of a bramble she rides now;
　Through brakes and through briers,
　O'er ditches and mires,
She follows the spirit that guides now.

No beast for his food
Dares now range the wood,
But hushed in his lair he lies lurking;
　While mischiefs by these,
　On lands and on seas,
At noon of night are a-working.

The storm will arise
And trouble the skies;

This night, and more for the wonder,
    The ghost from the tomb
    Affrighted shall come,
Called out by the clap of the thunder.

Not a great poet, Herrick excelled in small things, in sprightly
miniatures, in the significance of the insignificant. In his poems
are details which seem too unimportant to demand attention
yet which grow large in retrospect. It might be said that, more
than any other poet, Herrick trifled his way from offhand verse
to pure poetry.

Some of his pleasantest minuscule pieces are about children,
and the best of these are more touching than his most solemn
eulogies. This, for instance, is a four-line epitaph "Upon a
Child."

    Here a pretty baby lies
    Sung asleep with lullabies;
    Pray be silent, and not stir
    Th' easy earth that covers her.

Herrick never ceased to play with words. Even the lines he
intended to be cut on his tombstone are a quaint appeal "To a
Robin Redbreast," an appeal which mingles pathos with a sidelong pun on his first name.

    Laid out for dead, let thy last kindness be
    With leaves and moss-work for to cover me.
    And while the wood-nymphs my cold corpse inter,
    Sing thou my dirge, sweet-warbling chorister.
    For epitaph, in foliage, next write this:
    Here, here the tomb of Robin Herrick is.

Puritan Rebel

JOHN MILTON
[1608–1674]

A GREAT POET, John Milton was an equally great spirit, a dedicated fighter for freedom, a patriotic Puritan who rebelled against the corruption of his day. Of stubborn country stock, he was born in London December 9, 1608, during a period of violent political upheaval. His father had been disinherited because he could not accept the strictures of Catholicism and had become a Protestant. From his father, who supported himself by preparing documents and composing songs, Milton derived his love of music as well as his firmness. Shakespeare was still alive when Milton was playing in the streets near the Globe theater, and it is possible that the dramatist may have noticed a child of six because of his extraordinary beauty. It was a beauty that survived childhood.

When, at seventeen, after an improvement in the family fortunes, Milton attended Christ's College at Cambridge, his fellows teased him about his delicate features, fine eyes, fair complexion, and reddish hair. They nicknamed him "the lady of Christ's." He was, however, anything but effeminate. Years later, he wrote: "I was strong and capable enough in my youth to handle a weapon so that, wearing a sword by my side, I was a match for those that were much stronger."

Milton was not popular with his classmates; he was too serious to respond lightly to teasing. Books were his life. He said, "My father destined me, while yet a child, to the study and practice of literature." He quarreled with his teachers about the curriculum; he resented being made to compose academic compositions on dull subjects. As a result he was sent home for part of a term. Nevertheless, it was at Cambridge that he wrote some of his remarkable early poems: "On May Morning," "The Passion," "At a Solemn Music," an ode "On the Morning of Christ's Nativity," and the precocious, soul-searching sonnet, "On Arriving at the Age of Twenty-Three."

> How soon hath Time, the subtle thief of youth,
> Stolen on his wing my three-and-twentieth year!
> My hasting days fly on with full career,
> But my late spring no bud or blossom shew'th.[1]
> Perhaps my semblance might deceive the truth
> That I to manhood am arrived so near;
> And inward ripeness doth much less appear,
> That some more timely-happy spirits endu'th.[2]
>
> Yet be it less or more, or soon or slow,
> It shall be still in strictest measure even
> To that same lot, however mean or high,
> Toward which Time leads me, and the will of Heaven.
> All is, if I have grace to use it so,
> As ever in my great Taskmaster's eye.

It was also at Cambridge before he was twenty-three that Milton wrote "On Shakespeare." The poem marked his first appearance in print, and it had the distinction of being published as a preface to the second folio of Shakespeare's plays.

> What needs my Shakespeare for his honored bones,
> The labor of an age in pilèd stones?
> Or that his hallowed reliques should be hid
> Under a star-ypointing pyramid?

[1] Shows. [2] Endows.

> Dear son of memory, great heir of fame,
> What need'st thou such weak witness of thy name?
> Thou in our wonder and astonishment
> Hast built thyself a livelong monument.
> For whilst, to the shame of slow-endeavoring art,
> Thy easy numbers flow, and that each heart
> Hath from the leaves of thy unvalued book
> Those Delphic lines with deep impression took;
> Then thou, our fancy of itself bereaving,
> Dost make us marble with too much conceiving,
> And so sepulchred in such pomp dost lie
> That kings for such a tomb would wish to die.

His father had intended that his son should enter the church, but Milton's rebellious nature could not tolerate authority, even ecclesiastical. Nor was he interested in the law, his father's second choice. Instead, he occupied himself reading and writing at his father's estate at Horton. "I enjoyed," he said, "an interval of uninterrupted leisure, which I devoted to the study of Greek and Latin authors, although I occasionally visited the metropolis either for the sake of purchasing books or of learning something new in mathematics or in music." The "interval of uninterrupted leisure" lasted almost six years.

At Horton he wrote the most famous of all matching poems, "L'Allegro" (The Merry Man) and "Il Penseroso" (The Melancholy Man). The first is a morning hymn to happiness; the second is an evening meditation. "L'Allegro" is all light and happiness; the syllables leap and dance with unrestrained gaiety. The plowman whistles, the milkmaid sings, the mower sharpens his scythe, the cock crows—his "lively din scatters the rear of darkness thin"—merry bells ring out, "jocund rebecks" (lively fiddles) play, and everything echoes with mirth, with

> Jest and youthful jollity,
> Quips and cranks and wanton wiles,
> Nods and becks and wreathèd smiles . . .
> Sport that wrinkled care derides
> And laughter holding both its sides.

"L'Allegro" is a continuous response to a holiday mood, a mood that includes "the busy hum of men," the pride of "towered cities," of pomp, plays, and poetry. Milton recalls Ben Jonson's dramas, hears

> . . . sweetest Shakespeare, Fancy's child,
> Warble his native wood-notes wild . . .

and ends:

> These delights if thou canst give,
> Mirth, with thee I mean to live.

Both poems have the same number of syllables in each line, but, whereas those of "L'Allegro" trip along with nimble airiness, those of "Il Penseroso" are heavily weighted. The pace of the second is slow, the beat is retarded to suggest serious contemplation. There is the sad voice of the nightingale singing in the night, the sound of a distant waterfall as the speaker, wrapped in his silent thoughts, watches the stars bring all heaven before his eyes. The spirit of "Il Penseroso" is in such lines as:

> Come, pensive Nun, devout and pure,
> Sober, steadfast, and demure,
> All in a robe of darkest grain
> Flowing with majestic train,
> And sable stole of cypress lawn
> Over thy decent shoulders drawn.
> Come, but keep thy wonted state,
> With even step, and musing gait,
> And looks commercing with the skies,
> Thy rapt soul sitting in thine eyes.

Milton's happiness at Horton is apparent in what he did during that period. He put his leisure to good use. Besides "L'Allegro" and "Il Penseroso," he wrote two charming masques, "Arcades" and "Comus." The masque was much favored as an entertainment at the royal court and private palaces. It was a combination of pomp and pageantry, opera and drama. Usually pastoral in background, it also contained an allegory, a double meaning with a half-hidden moral. "Comus" unfolded what became Milton's favorite theme: the conflict between Good and Evil, in which after much temptation, virtue inevitably triumphed. It was performed with elaborate settings, brilliant music, and lasting poetry. Had Milton never written anything more than what he had accomplished by the time he was twenty-six, he would have to be ranked among the major poets. But his great masterpieces were still ahead of him.

"Lycidas" was written before he was thirty. Although Milton had never been intimate with any of his classmates, there was one whose short life he remembered and whose early death he immortalized. This was Edward King, who intended to become a minister and who, at twenty-eight, perished at sea on a visit to his family in Ireland. "Lycidas" is in the form of a pastoral elegy, a lament and an appeal to the Muses that Milton's dead friend be recognized by the hosts of heaven ("Look homeward, Angel") and his memory be cherished by men. The poem is a combination (and, to some, a confusion) of Christian and pagan allusions, but its nobility and beauty lift it above its sometimes puzzling references.

At thirty Milton completed his education by visiting Italy. The fame of his Latin poems had preceded him, and he was acclaimed by artists and poets who dedicated poems to him. In Florence he talked with Galileo, the scientist who had challenged the teachings of his predecessors, and went on to Rome and Naples, where again he was much honored. He was about to extend his tour when disturbing news reached him. Relations between King Charles and his subjects had grown steadily worse; the threat of civil war was in the air; and Milton abruptly returned home. "I thought it base to be traveling for amusement," he said, "while my fellow citizens were fighting for liberty at home."

When civil war broke out Milton did not hesitate to declare himself. He was on the side of the struggling democracy and the people against a dissipated monarch and tyrannical power. He wrote pamphlets calling for Queen Truth as opposed to King Charles. Cromwell, the militant leader of the new order, made Milton, its fervent champion, Latin Secretary of State. The poet stopped writing poetry and, for a long time, wrote only in prose. He brought all his energy and learning to his aid, saying, "When God commands to take the trumpet and blow a dolorous or jarring blast, it lies not in man's will what he shall say or what he shall conceal."

In the midst of his attacks on the divine right of kings, to everyone's surprise, Milton married a seventeen-year-old girl. It was not a happy union. Mary Powell had been brought up in a Royalist household to enjoy the lighter side of life. Unlike her serious Puritan husband, who was seventeen years older than herself, she was fond of light pleasures, parties, and games. When she went home for what was to be a short visit to her parents, she refused to return. She remained away almost four years, and only the triumph of Cromwell brought her back to Milton, accompanied by her whole family as refugees. She begged his mercy and received it. Meekly she obeyed him and, after the birth of her fourth child, died at twenty-six.

Milton continued to fight for the freedoms which to him were most important: the right of men to live at liberty, the right to be liberally educated, and the right to speak and write freely. He was particularly eloquent about the protection of publications against censorship or "starched conformity." He declared that while it is wrong to kill a man, it is worse to kill a book. He argued this way: "Who kills a man kills a reasonable creature, God's image. But he who destroys a book kills reason itself, kills the image of God. . . . Many a man lives a burden to the earth; but a good book is the precious life-blood of a master-spirit, embalmed and treasured up on purpose to a life beyond life."

During the years of research and the writing of long pamphlets, his eyesight, weak at the best, grew much worse. In his mid-forties he became totally blind. Doctors had told him that he was putting too much strain on his eyes, but he ignored their warnings. "The choice lay between dereliction of a supreme duty and loss of eyesight," he wrote. "If my affliction is incurable, I prepare myself and compose myself accordingly." His composure strengthened the determination to continue work. It is expressed in what has become his most often quoted poem, "On His Blindness," a stoic triumph of resignation.

> When I consider how my light is spent
> Ere half my days in this dark world and wide,
> And that one talent which is death to hide
> Lodged with me useless, though my soul more bent
> To serve therewith my Maker, and present
> My true account, lest He returning chide,
> "Doth God exact day-labor, light denied?"
> I fondly ask. But Patience, to prevent
> That murmur, soon replies, "God doth not need
> Either man's work or his own gifts. Who best
> Bear his mild yoke, they serve him best. His state
> Is kingly: thousands at his bidding speed,
> And post o'er land and ocean without rest;
> They also serve who only stand and wait."

In his mid-fifties Milton began his far-reaching masterpiece, the epical *Paradise Lost.* Since he was blind, he could not write but had to dictate line after line. He depended largely on his three daughters, only one of whom was wholly cooperative. The others rebelled against the daily drudgery. He had married three times—after two years of marriage, his second wife, like his first, had died of childbirth. He was aging rapidly. The once auburn hair was gray; his expression was lifeless; his eyes were dead of everything except an inner vision.

It was the inner vision which allowed Milton to complete his vast concept. Since he considered rhyme too pretty for so colossal a project, he discarded it in favor of the rolling richness of blank verse. *Paradise Lost,* as the title indicates, has as its theme the Fall of Man. It begins with the story of "man's first disobedience"; its object is to "justify the ways of God to man." In the midst of the conflict between the power of good and the persistence of evil there are exquisite passages. None is more touching than the lyrical episode when, as night comes on, Adam and Eve approach their bower. In this tender moment, and in accents of adoration, Eve speaks:

With thee conversing, I forget all time,
All seasons, and their change, all please alike.
Sweet is the breath of morn, her rising sweet,
With charm of earliest birds; pleasant the sun,
When first on this delightful land he spreads
His orient beams, on herb, tree, fruit, and flower,
Glistering with dew; fragrant the fertile earth
After soft showers; and sweet the coming-on
Of grateful evening mild; then silent night,
With this her solemn bird, and this fair moon,
And these the gems of heaven, her starry train.
But neither breath of morn, when she ascends
With charm of earliest birds; nor rising sun
On this delightful land; nor herb, fruit, flower
Glistering with dew; nor fragrance after showers;
Nor grateful evening mild; nor silent night,
With this her solemn bird; nor walk by moon,
Or glittering starlight, without thee is sweet.

The style throughout *Paradise Lost* is worthy of its theme.
Matthew Arnold said that, more than any other poet, Milton
represented "the grand manner" in English poetry. Concluding
with the expulsion from Eden, the twelve books of the poem
end in quiet majesty.

The Archangel stood, and from the other hill
To their fixed station, all in bright array,
The cherubim descended, on the ground
Gliding meteorous, as evening mist
Risen from a river o'er the marish[1] glides,
And gathers ground fast at the laborer's heel
Homeward returning. High in front advanced,
The brandished sword of God before them blazed,
Fierce as a comet; which with torrid heat
And vapor as the Libyan air adust,[2]
Began to parch that temperate clime. Whereat
In either hand the hastening Angel caught

[1] An old spelling of marsh. [2] The heat of the Archangel's sword had scorched
the Garden and turned it into dust.

Our lingering parents, and to the eastern gate
Led them direct, and down the cliff as fast
To the subjected plain—then disappeared.
They, looking back, all the eastern side beheld
Of Paradise, so late their happy seat,
Waved over by that flaming brand; the gate
With dreadful faces thronged and fiery arms.
Some natural tears they dropped, but wiped them soon.
The world was all before them, where to choose
Their place of rest, and Providence their guide.
They, hand in hand, with wandering steps and slow,
Through Eden took their solitary way.

In spite of Milton's idealism, it seemed that the people cared
little for self-government. Cromwell died about ten years after
Charles I had been beheaded, and English men and women
enthusiastically welcomed the return of monarchy in the person
of the frivolous Charles II. Milton was forced to go into hiding.
In spite of his plea about the sacredness of books, his own books
were burned in public and he was in danger of being executed.
Thanks to the influence of a few fellow-poets, he was pardoned,
released, and was able to resume writing. He published *Paradise Regained,* a sequel to *Paradise Lost,* and an eloquent
but undramatic play, *Samson Agonistes.* He busied himself
with a history of Britain, a Latin grammar, and a book on logic.

His last days were plagued with gout, but he was able to
enjoy the music of the organ, which he still could play. He gave
permission to the poet John Dryden to turn *Paradise Lost*
into an opera. He was sixty-six when, on November 8, 1674, he
died. He slipped out of life so quietly that "the time of expiring
was not perceived by those in the room." Only a few of his
contemporaries paid tribute to the man whom later generations
were to hail as "the incomparable Milton." One critic of the
day referred to him as "a blind old man who wrote Latin
documents."

It must be confessed that Milton is not an altogether lovable
poet. His aloofness, his lack of humor, his very elevated tone

command our respect without winning our instant affection. But there can be no question about his grandeur. He compels our admiration not only by his purpose but by the sheer power of his lines. He may not be a companionable figure, a man for every mood, but he has magnificence. Like his hero-villain Satan,

> He above the rest,
> In shape and gesture proudly eminent,
> Stood like a tower.

Immortal Wit

ALEXANDER POPE

[1688–1744]

IT IS A HIDEOUS IRONY that the genius who perfected the shape-liest verse ever written in English was a misshapen dwarf. He had a few admiring friends who made excuses for him, and an army of enemies who forgave him nothing. Those whom he offended in his satires—a formidable lot—considered him "an evil little carcass," "a wicked wasp," "a human gadfly," "a gargoyle of a man."

When Alexander Pope was born in London, May 21, 1688, he was not merely a normal but a handsome baby. At the age of twelve, however, a severe illness ruined his health and left him deformed. He grew up intellectually but not physically; he remained less than four and a half feet high, a twisted, under-size cripple.

He was further handicapped by being a Roman Catholic at a time when Catholics could not hold public office or even attend the universities. Moreover, he was the son of a small merchant, a commoner, in a period when titles were the cus-tomary way of advancing a career. Nevertheless, Pope was per-sistent as well as precocious. He made rhymes ("numbers") as soon as he could talk, and when he began to write, verses flowed more fluently than prose. Many years later, when he spoke of "this long disease, my life," he remembered the ease with which he had turned to poetry.

> As yet a child, nor yet a fool to fame,
> I lisped in numbers, for the numbers came.

It was just after illness struck him that he wrote one of his most often quoted poems. "Solitude" seems a strange poem for a twelve-year-old boy to have written, but it owed its origin to two things: the shock from which he suffered and the solace he gained from reading. The sentiment expressed in these lines was suggested by a Latin poem, one of Horace's epodes, but the treatment is that of a prodigy who, not yet in his teens, was already a skilled technician.

> Happy the man, whose wish and care
> A few paternal acres bound,
> Content to breathe his native air
>   In his own ground.

> Whose herds with milk, whose fields with bread,
> Whose flocks supply him with attire;
> Whose trees in summer yield him shade,
>   In winter, fire.

> Blest, who can unconcernedly find
> Hours, days, and years slide soft away
> In health of body, peace of mind:
>   Quiet by day.

> Sound sleep by night; study and ease
> Together mixed, sweet recreation,
> And innocence, which most does please
>   With meditation.

> Thus let me live, unseen, unknown;
> Thus unlamented let me die,
> Steal from the world, and not a stone
>   Tell where I lie.

Between his twelfth and fifteenth years Pope wrote an epic poem of some four thousand lines, and, at sixteen, a series of

Pastorals which were circulated in manuscript and caught the attention of some of the celebrities of the day. One of them, Sir George Granville, enthusiastically proclaimed his discovery: "His name is Pope. He is not above seventeen or eighteen and promises miracles. If he goes on, as he has begun, in the pastoral way, as Virgil first tried his strength, we may hope to see English poetry vie with the Roman."

Pope was barely twenty-one when four of the pastorals, together with an adaptation from Chaucer, were printed in Tonson's *Miscellany*. A distinguished audience welcomed them, and after that public debut, there was no doubt about Pope's fame.

In his early twenties Pope met the Blount sisters, Teresa and Martha, and, though he wrote tender poems to Teresa, it was Martha who became his dearest friend and lifelong companion. At twenty-three he enlarged his reputation with the publication of *An Essay on Criticism,* which enlivened the usual dull subject of poetic rules and critical judgments with couplets as terse and tight as two-line epigrams. For example:

> A little learning is a dangerous thing;
> Drink deep, or taste not the Pierian spring.

> Be not the first by whom the new are tried,
> Nor yet the last to lay the old aside.

> A perfect judge will read each work of wit
> With the same spirit that its author writ.

> Whoever thinks a faultless piece to see,
> Thinks what ne'er was, nor is, nor e'er shall be.

An Essay on Criticism went on to make fun of the padding and the clichés that were current in the fashionable poetry of the period.

> While expletives their feeble aid do join
> And ten low words oft creep in one dull line:
> While they ring round the same unvaried chimes,
> With sure returns of still expected rhymes:

Where'er you find "the cooling western breeze,"
In the next line it "whispers through the trees,"
If crystal streams "with pleasing murmurs creep,"
The reader's threatened (not in vain) with "sleep."

Pope then proceeded to suggest the art as well as the craft of writing, and gave examples of both:

True ease in writing comes from art, not chance,
As those move easiest who have learned to dance.
'Tis not enough no harshness gives offence;
The sound must seem an Echo to the sense:
Soft is the strain when Zephyr gently blows,
And the smooth stream in smoother numbers flows;
But when loud surges lash the sounding shore,
The hoarse, rough verse should like the torrent roar:
When Ajax strives some rock's vast weight to throw,
The line too labors, and the words move slow;
Not so, when swift Camilla scours the plain,
Flies o'er the unbending corn, and skims along the main.

There were a few jibes in *An Essay on Criticism* at mediocre poets and dramatists. One of them was directed against John Dennis, and although the barb was not too sharply pointed, Dennis acted as though the sting had been intended as a mortal wound. Dennis retaliated in the most shameful way. He called attention to Pope's unfortunate deformity, cruelly ridiculed his defects, compared him to a monkey, and implied that had Pope been born in Grecian times, his father would not have permitted such a monstrosity to live.

It was the first of many sneers, slights, and hurts that Pope had to endure. No wonder he struck back and, anticipating an attack, struck before his adversary could deliver the blow. His self-assertiveness was a form of self-defense, an overcompensation for a sensitive nature made extra-sensitive because of his inability to fight except with words. He seldom acknowledged the depth of his wounds. Yet, in the midst of a lighthearted letter to John Gay, author of much light verse, Pope alluded to his pain.

So the struck deer in some sequestered part
Lies down to die, the arrow at her heart:
There, stretched unseen to coverts hid from day,
Bleeds drop by drop, and pants his life away.

The eighteenth-century critic and poet Samuel Johnson said that Pope was always frail but that in middle age he was so weak that he could not even dress himself and that he had to wear a kind of stiff bodice, being unable to stand until it was laced tight. He could never hold his body erect. "One side was contracted," said Johnson. "His legs were so slender that he enlarged their bulk with three pairs of stockings which were drawn on and off by the maid. He neither went to bed nor rose without help."

Pope's associations with men were usually unfortunate; his relations with most women were disastrous. Quarrels with them led to bitter recriminations. The aristocratic Lady Montagu let it be known that Pope had dared to make love to her and that she had repulsed him "in an immoderate fit of laughter." Pope might have pardoned her rejection of him, but the laughter was something he could not forgive. He branded Lady Montagu in poem after poem, called her miserly, not to be trusted in financial matters, mean to her sister, neglectful of her child. He blackened her reputation in every possible way, repeatedly, remorselessly.

His most brilliant poem, *The Rape of the Lock,* brought about further unhappy involvements. The person to whom it was dedicated, a popular beauty named Arabella Fermor, was offended because she felt she had been caricatured. Her friends sided with her and attacked the author of the poem as well as the poem itself, which is a mock-epic, a delightfully gay satire on a foolish, self-loving society. The essayist William Hazlitt wrote that reading *The Rape of the Lock* was like "looking at the world through a microscope, where everything assumes a new character, where the little becomes gigantic. . . . It is a triumph of insignificance, the apotheosis of frippery and folly."

At twenty-seven Pope was in need of money to support himself even in a modest way. It was then that he began a translation of Homer's *Iliad*. It took six years and the help of four assistants to complete and was so successful that he never again had to concern himself about finances. Pope's version of the Greek epic was praised for its rapid pace and fluent readability, but one critic voiced the opinion of classical scholars when he wrote, "A fine poem, Mr. Pope, but you must not call it Homer."

This time Pope did not lose his temper. He could afford to smile, for readers liked his dexterous mannerisms and made much of them and him. He was the man of the hour. He was thirty-one when he bought a villa at Twickenham, where he spent the rest of his life. Twickenham became a meeting place for illustrious lords and ladies. Writers as eminent as Swift and Voltaire honored Pope with visits; politicians came to talk poetry as well as politics. In short, Pope was treated as though he were a royal personage living in luxurious retirement.

In spite of the pleasures of his country retreat, Pope could not stay idle. He composed various epistles, edited the works of Shakespeare, and, as a sequel to the *Iliad,* published his translation of the *Odyssey.* At forty he began *The Dunciad,* a long poem against dunces (as the title implied), against dullness, and against all those who had troubled, teased, or tormented him. It amused many and offended many more, for, besides its attack on individuals, it made biting fun of all the fads and social follies of the day. Pope could not help but be pleased by the furor started by *The Dunciad.* "I had little thought three months ago to have drawn the whole polite world upon me," he wrote—and then went on to add another even more sarcastic section.

In his mid-forties Pope was busier than ever. He had much to do with dozens of books, pamphlets, and poems. The "Epistle to Eloisa" is a surprisingly tender declaration. "It grows warm and begins to have some breathings of the heart in it," he wrote to Martha Blount, "which may make posterity think I was in love." Posterity was surely in Pope's mind when he wrote the lines which have been as often quoted as though they were Gospel: *An Essay on Man.*

An Essay on Man is not a profound piece of philosophy.

It was not meant to be. Pope's intention was "to contribute some honest and moral purposes in writing on human life and manners, not exclusive of religious regards, and I have many fragments which I am beginning to put together." The *Essay* justified his purpose. It is, as he indicated, a chain of "fragments," but its bits and pieces make such lively reading that we forget how fragmentary the poem actually is. Never had rhymed couplets been so trimmed and sharpened, so delicately turned and so pointed with wit. Here are a few excerpts:

> Know then thyself; presume not God to scan;
> The proper study of mankind is man.

> Whate'er the passion—knowledge, fame or pelf—
> No one will change his neighbor with himself.

> Honor and shame from no condition rise;
> Act well your part, there all the honor lies.

> Laugh where we must; be candid where we can;
> But vindicate the ways of God to man.

> Hope springs eternal in the human breast;
> Man never is, but always to be blest.

> A wit's a feather, and a chief a rod;
> An honest man's the noblest work of God.

> Behold the child, by nature's kindly law,
> Pleased with a rattle, tickled with a straw:
> Some livelier plaything gives his youth delight,
> A little louder, but as empty quite.
> Scarfs, garters, gold, amuse his riper stage,
> And beads and prayer-books are the toys of age.
> Pleased with this bauble still, as that before;
> Till tired he sleeps, and life's poor play is o'er.

Although Pope's health grew worse in his fifties, he never stopped working. He enlarged the *Dunciad*, edited his literary correspondence, published *Imitations of Horace,* and planned a *History of the Rise and Progress of English Poetry.* As his pains increased, he grew concerned for his life. He was so weak that he wrote to a friend, "If your charity would take up a small bird that is half dead and set it chirping for half an hour, I will jump into my cage and put myself in your hands. Two horses will be enough to draw me—so would two dogs." His last letter was written to the faithful Martha Blount. "In bed, or sitting, it hurts my breast. In the afternoon I can do nothing, still less by candlelight. . . . I have little to say to you when we meet, but I love you upon unalterable principles." A few days after his fifty-sixth birthday, on May 30, 1744, he died.

A perfect exponent of his age, an age of cultivated irony and extreme sophistication, of affectation rather than true sentiment, Pope went out of fashion shortly after his death. The romantic nineteenth century found him "dated"; his cleverness was admitted, but he was thought of as nothing more than a nimble versifier, an essayist with a gift of rhyme. The twentieth century reversed this estimate and restored him to a place of honor.

Today he is admired not only for his brilliant technique but for the way in which he lifted commonplaces to unforgettable utterances. He anticipated the talk-flavored poems of Wordsworth and Frost; he casually created phrases that have become proverbs for all time. Our language would have been poorer without such phrasings as "To err is human; to forgive divine"; "Fools rush in where angels fear to tread"; "Order is Heaven's first law"; "Whatever is, is right"; "Damn with faint praise"; "What so tedious as a twice-told tale?"; "Who shall decide when doctors disagree"; "Guide, philosopher, and friend."

The cruel attacks, the malice and misfortunes no longer matter and can be forgotten. The wit and precision of the lines will live as long as English is spoken.

Pure Vision

WILLIAM BLAKE
[1757–1827]

WILLIAM BLAKE'S vivid imagination pierced every surface and let him see the life that throbs in seemingly lifeless matter, the energy concealed in things too small to notice, the immense within the minute. He voiced this thought again and again, notably (and, judging from anthologies, most quotably) in the first four lines of his "Auguries of Innocence":

> To see a World in a grain of sand
> And a Heaven in a wild flower,
> Hold Infinity in the palm of your hand
> And Eternity in an hour.

Blake was born November 28, 1757, son of a hosier, and was a visionary almost from birth. He was four years old when he screamed that he saw God put his forehead against the window. When he was about eight he came home from a walk in the fields and reported that he had seen a tree full of angels, "their bright angelic wings bespangling every bough with stars." His was not only a poetic but also a prophetic vision. When Blake was still a boy, his father took him to the studio of the artist William Ryland. The boy was uncomfortable and wanted to leave. "Father," he said afterward, "I do not like that man's

90

face. It is the face of a man who is going to be hanged." Twelve years later Ryland was hanged.

Blake never went to school. He absorbed knowledge from everything about him. Not until he was fourteen did his father show concern about his son's inclination to substitute fantasy for reality. He thereupon planned for his future. Apprenticed to an engraver, Blake found his way from commerce to art, and from art to literature. It was his own way. In his twelfth year Blake had written some remarkably inspired poetry. Before he was twenty he had composed a set of poems as spontaneous as the lyrics of the Elizabethan poets. These early *Poetical Sketches* are as direct as children's rhymes, but they are transformed by an intensity which is both simple and tender and sometimes sublime. "My silks and fine array," "How sweet I roamed," and "To the Evening Star" are a few of the loveliest.

MY SILKS AND FINE ARRAY

My silks and fine array,
　My smiles and languished air,
By love are driven away;
　And mournful lean Despair
Brings me yew to deck my grave;
Such end true lovers have.

His face is fair as heaven
　When springing buds unfold;
Oh, why to him was't given,
　Whose heart is wintry cold?
His breast is love's all-worshiped tomb
Where all love's pilgrims come.

Bring me an axe and spade,
　Bring me a winding-sheet;
When I my grave have made,
　Let winds and tempests beat:
Then down I'll lie, as cold as clay.
True love doth pass away!

HOW SWEET I ROAMED

How sweet I roamed from field to field
  And tasted all the summer's pride,
Till I the prince of love beheld
  Who in the sunny beams did glide!

He showed me lilies for my hair,
  And blushing roses for my brow;
He led me through his gardens fair
  Where all his golden pleasures grow.

With sweet May dews my wings were wet,
  And Phoebus fired my vocal rage;
He caught me in his silken net,
  And shut me in his golden cage.

He loves to sit and hear me sing,
  Then, laughing, sports and plays with me;
Then stretches out my golden wing,
  And mocks my loss of liberty.

TO THE EVENING STAR

Thou fair-haired angel of the evening
Now, whilst the sun rests on the mountains, light
Thy bright torch of love; thy radiant crown
Put on, and smile upon our evening bed!
Smile on our loves, and, while thou drawest the
Blue curtains of the sky, scatter thy silver dew
On every flower that shuts its sweet eyes
In timely sleep. Let thy west wind sleep on
The lake; speak silence with thy glimmering eyes,
And wash the dusk with silver. Soon, full soon,
Dost thou withdraw; then the wolf rages wide,
And the lion glares through the dun forest:
The fleeces of our flocks are covered with
Thy sacred dew: protect them with thine influence.

Blake was an impulsive, burning-eyed man not yet twenty-five
when he fell in love with Catherine Boucher, the beautiful,

twenty-year-old daughter of a gardener. His courtship was as curious as it was brief. Immediately upon meeting her, he told how he had been mocked by another girl, and when Catherine sympathized with him, he asked, "Then you pity me?" "Indeed I do," she replied. "Then," declared Blake, "I love you." A marriage took place soon after, and the two remained quietly but unalterably in love the rest of their lives. Although she was lovely, Catherine was almost illiterate. Unable to spell, she had to put a cross in front of her name on the marriage register. It was Blake who taught her to read and write. Patient, adaptable, and undemanding, she was the ideal wife for a dreaming idealist. When a friend inquired what kept Blake occupied so much of the time, she replied, "I have very little of Mr. Blake's company. He is always in Paradise."

With the help of his younger brother Robert, and aided by Catherine, William opened a bookshop to sell prints, his own as well as others. It was not a successful venture. The scheme collapsed in little more than a year when Robert died. Blake was grief-stricken but would not be embittered either for Robert or himself—he said he had seen Robert's soul rise from the body "clapping its hands for joy."

With Catherine's help, Blake designed and issued his writings in books different in form from anything hitherto printed. The books were not set up in the ordinary method but were lettered and decorated by hand in acid-proof ink on metal plates. The plates were then put into basins filled with acid, and the parts not covered with the acid-proof ink were eaten away. After the acid bath the lettering (which had to be drawn backward so as to be readable when the sheets of paper were printed) and the decorations stood out boldly. Then Blake and his wife printed the pages and colored them, each book being slightly different from the others in its finished form. Only two of Blake's many works were produced in the conventional way.

The designs were not meant to be mere decorations. Blake considered them as important as the words. Aiming to unite the lettering with the designs, Blake intertwined them with flowerlike backgrounds. He conceived of the poems as part of the designs; one did not exist without the other.

Blake was thirty-two when he issued what became his best-known work, *Songs of Innocence*. At first it was thought to be intended for children, for the first poem concluded with this stanza:

> And I made a rural pen,
> And I stained the water clear,
> And I wrote my happy songs
> Every child may joy to hear.

They are indeed happy songs, and any child might "joy to hear" them. But Blake was thinking of the child in every man, and he thought of innocence as the spirit of happiness and freedom which can come at any age. Artless though the lines seem to be, they are symbolic as well as simple. For example, "The Little Black Boy" expresses the hope for brotherly love to break down racial prejudice; when Blake speaks of the lamb's meekness and mildness, he makes us think of the meek and blessed innocence of the Lamb of God.

THE LITTLE BLACK BOY

My mother bore me in the southern wild,
And I am black, but O! my soul is white;
White as an angel is the English child,
But I am black, as if bereaved of light.

My mother taught me underneath a tree,
And, sitting down before the heat of day,
She took me on her lap and kissèd me,
And, pointing to the east, began to say:

"Look on the rising sun—there God does live,
And gives his light, and gives his heat away;
And flowers and trees and beasts and men receive
Comfort in morning, joy in the noon day.

"And we are put on earth a little space,
That we may learn to bear the beams of love;
And these black bodies and this sunburnt face
Is but a cloud, and like a shady grove.

"For when our souls have learned the heat to bear,
The cloud will vanish, we shall hear his voice,
Saying: 'Come out from the grove, my love and care,
And round my golden tent like lambs rejoice.'"

Thus did my mother say, and kissèd me;
And thus I say to little English boy.
When I from black, and he from white cloud free,
And round the tent of God like lambs we joy,

I'll shade him from the heat, till he can bear
To lean in joy upon our father's knee;
And then I'll stand and stroke his silver hair,
And be like him, and he will then love me.

THE LAMB

Little Lamb, who made thee?
Dost thou know who made thee;
Gave thee life and bid thee feed
By the stream and o'er the mead;
Gave thee such a tender voice
Making all the vales rejoice?
Little Lamb, who made thee?
Dost thou know who made thee?

Little Lamb, I'll tell thee,
Little Lamb, I'll tell thee:
He is callèd by thy name,
For He calls Himself a Lamb.
He is meek and He is mild;
He became a little child.
I a child and thou a lamb,
We are callèd by His name.
Little Lamb, God bless thee.
Little Lamb, God bless thee.

Blake was not content to present only one side of the picture.
Human joy has its opposite in sadness; good is opposed by evil.

It was inevitable that Blake's *Songs of Innocence* would be succeeded by *Songs of Experience*. Published five years after *Songs of Innocence, Songs of Experience* was presented with this motto: "Without contraries is no progression." According to Blake, experience shows us that life is a continual conflict of give and take, a pairing of opposites (or "contraries"), of good and evil, of innocence and experience, of body and soul. The mild Lamb is contrasted with the ferocious Tiger ("burning bright/ In the forests of the night") yet both are beautiful, both are a part of the natural world, both have been created by God's "immortal hand or eye."

THE TIGER

Tiger! Tiger! burning bright
In the forests of the night,
What immortal hand or eye
Could frame thy fearful symmetry?

In what distant deeps or skies
Burnt the fire of thine eyes?
On what wings dare he aspire?
What the hand dare seize the fire!

And what shoulder, and what art,
Could twist the sinews of thy heart?
And when thy heart began to beat,
What dread hand? and what dread feet?

What the hammer? what the chain?
In what furnace was thy brain?
What the anvil? what dread grasp
Dare its deadly terrors clasp?

When the stars threw down their spears
And watered heaven with their tears,
Did he smile his work to see?
Did he who made the Lamb make thee?

> Tiger! Tiger! burning bright
> In the forests of the night,
> What immortal hand or eye
> Dare frame thy fearful symmetry?

It was not easy for Blake to support himself and his wife. He had the greatest difficulty selling his own highly original engravings and had to engrave the designs of more popular artists to make a living. A show of his imaginative paintings failed. The times were distinctly out of joint for Blake. He was by nature a nonconformer; he believed that no one should try to restrain the aspirations of the human spirit or put limitations on the imagination. Opposed to all forms of bondage, which he considered tyranny, Blake wrote:

> He who binds to himself a Joy
> Doth the wingèd life destroy;
> But he who kisses the Joy as it flies
> Lives in Eternity's sunrise.

Blake was always for freshness of thought. He distrusted what was fashionable, fought the conventions which repressed the poor, and continually questioned the manner in which the society of his time ruled the world. His writings responded to the revolutionary spirit that was affecting the age in which he lived. Revolution itself was in the air. The American Revolution and the French Revolution were followed by the Industrial Revolution when machinery began to take the place of men.

Blake rebelled against anything like a machine-like civilization with its worship of power expressed in its worship of money. He said scornfully:

> Can Wisdom be put in a silver rod?
> Or Love in a golden bowl?

Blake put his dissenting ideas into a series of prophetic books. Among them were such strange and startling works as *Europe: A Prophecy, The First Book of Urizen, The Book of Los, The Four Zoas, America: A Prophecy, The Marriage of Heaven and*

Hell. Much of these works was disturbing, much was unintelligible to most readers. But Blake was not being mystical for the sake of mystery. He cut through the surface, the outer show, to the inner being, the creative core. "Enthusiastic admiration is the first principle of knowledge," he announced in one of his concise adages.

It is in sudden glimpses that we comprehend Blake, not in literal interpretation, but in moments of revelation, in impressions and illuminations like the proverbs and epigrams in *The Marriage of Heaven and Hell.*

> The busy bee hath no time for sorrow.
>
> No bird soars too high if he soars with his own wings.
>
> One thought fills immensity.
>
> The cistern contains; the fountain overflows.
>
> You never know what is enough unless you know what is more than enough.
>
> Exuberance is Beauty.
>
> What is now proved was once only imagined.

When Blake was in his mid-thirties he and his wife found a small house in what was then the countryside, the village of Lambeth outside of London. They were happy there. It was an idyllic retreat, with a pleasant garden, a rustic arbor with a flourishing grapevine which, though it needed pruning, Blake refused to prune. He saw it as a symbol of onward-reaching and fruitfully rewarding life; therefore he would not cut back a single stem. The place was, for Blake and his wife, a simple Eden, and they lived there almost as naturally as Adam and Eve. A neighbor once saw them sitting unclothed in the garden. They were reading *Paradise Lost.*

For several years things went well there; Blake was unusually productive and, since he now had no trouble disposing of his designs, fairly prosperous. But Blake's nonconforming tendencies got him into trouble. He quarreled with influential friends, offended the authorities, and, when he threw an intruding soldier out of the garden, was charged with assaulting an officer and uttering seditious remarks. There was a trial for high treason and, though Blake was cleared of all charges, he was dispirited, especially when he no longer could count on sales of his work. No one took him seriously either as a poet or a painter. Critics found fault with the "fantastic and extravagant" conceptions of his engravings. A few collectors kept him and Catherine from starving.

Nevertheless, some of his largest works were done in the twenty years he had still to live. Blake considered *Milton*, the most ambitious of these, "an allegory for future generations" and maintained that, instead of laboring to produce it, it came as a prolonged inspiration, an almost automatic creation that wrote itself. "I may praise it," said Blake, "since I do not pretend to be any other than the secretary; the authors are in eternity." Even for scholars, *Milton* is difficult. It is a bewildering mixture of actual experiences and private associations, of the conscious and the unconscious. Perhaps the most ringing lines are those which conclude the Preface with a protest against the "dark satanic mills" of the factories and machines.

> And did those feet in ancient time
> Walk upon England's mountains green?
> And was the Holy Lamb of God
> On England's pleasant pastures seen?
>
> And did the countenance divine
> Shine forth upon our clouded hills?
> And was Jerusalem builded here
> Among these dark satanic mills?
>
> Bring me my bow of burning gold!
> Bring me my arrows of desire!
> Bring me my spear! O clouds, unfold!
> Bring me my chariot of fire!
>
> I will not cease from mental fight,
> Nor shall my sword sleep in my hand,
> Till we have built Jerusalem
> In England's green and pleasant land.

Blake continued to work and make his own mythology until the end. He was in his sixties when he began to suffer from overwork and impaired health. A few months before his death he wrote to a friend that though he was physically weak, the imagination was stronger than ever. He was busy illustrating Dante when he succumbed. "I have no grief in leaving you, Catherine," he had told his wife. "We have lived happily, we have lived long, we have been ever together." Saying he was going to the country that he had always wished to see, he died in his seventieth year on August 12, 1827. There was no public notice. The man who saw the world in a grain of sand was buried in an unmarked pauper's grave.

A few of Blake's contemporaries admitted his genius; most of them thought him mad. Today Blake is appreciated as one who penetrated the surface of reality and revealed the secret, elemental forces that govern life. Perhaps his greatest communications are not in the complicated prophetic books but in the smaller poems, in separate stanzas and proverbs. One can read and reread Blake's "Auguries of Innocence" for the power with which a series of random jottings convey their meaning with immediate effect. For example:

> A robin redbreast in a cage
> Puts all Heaven in a rage . . .
> A dog starved at his master's gate
> Predicts the ruin of the state . . .
> A skylark wounded in the wing,
> A cherubim does cease to sing . . .
> He who doubts from what he sees
> Will ne'er believe, do what you please.
> If the sun and moon should doubt,
> They'd immediately go out . . .
> We are led to believe a lie
> When we see with, not through, the eye.

Blake never wavered from his principles. He always saw through, not merely with, the eye. His was the eye of the true see-er, the seer, the pure visionary.

The Plowboy Poet

ROBERT BURNS
[1759-1796]

THE MOST POPULAR as well as the most naturally gifted Scottish poet, Robert Burns, was born January 25, 1759, in the village of Alloway near the town of Ayr. His childhood home was a rundown cottage built by his father, a poverty-driven farmer. Nine people—seven children and the two parents—slept in two rooms (plus a bed in the kitchen), crowded quarters which, from time to time, also housed various animals. The boy had little time for school. Fortunately, however, a teacher who boarded with the farmers taught Robert not only to read but also to appreciate what he was reading. It is said that the youth so loved the sound of rhyme and rhythm that, when he went to work in the fields, he took a collection of English lyrics with him.

In a way Burns was brought up on poetry. He imbibed it partly from the village schoolmaster and partly from an old lady, his mother's cousin, who told fantastic stories of fairies, witches, enchanted towers, dragons, and legendary heroes, all of which he never forgot and which, he said, "cultivated the latent seeds of poetry."

By the time he reached his teens the boy had to do the work of a man. His father, a makeshift farmer at the best, suffered the first of a series of breakdowns, and Robert became the prin-

101

cipal laborer. He had to move from one poor farm to another, each new one less productive and more unprofitable than the one he had left. He described himself as "a galley-slave," although his hardships were somewhat alleviated by the realization that he could put his troubles into song. He had fitted words to a tune sung by a fourteen-year-old girl who was working with him at harvest time and was delighted to find how easily the thoughts found the words that went so rightly with the melody. "Thus, with me," he wrote later, "began Love and Poesy, which at times have been my only and my highest enjoyment."

Burns had fallen in love at fifteen and he never fell out of it. He admitted that *Omnia vincit amor* (Love conquers everything) was all the Latin he knew. It was as a plowboy he wrote: "To the sons and daughters of labor and poverty, the ardent hope, the stolen interview, the tender farewell, are the greatest and the most delicious enjoyments." Although he was constantly in love, he was a most inconstant lover. Among his sweethearts were Nelly Kilpatrick, the "Handsome Nell" who inspired his first love poem; Alison Begbie, a servant girl, his "Bonnie Peggy Alison"; Mary Campbell, a dairymaid whom he immortalized in "Highland Mary"; Mary Morrison, to whom he dedicated one of his loveliest songs; Anne Park, the beautiful barmaid whose golden locks and melting form he celebrated in "Anna"; and the nineteen-year-old Jean Armour, whom he met when he was twenty-six and whom he eventually married. Perhaps the purest of his lyrics is the sixteen-line poem to Jean.

> Of a' the airts[1] the wind can blaw,
>   I dearly like the west,
> For there the bonnie lassie lives,
>   The lassie I lo'e best:
> There's wild woods grow, and rivers row,
>   And mony a hill between;
> But day and night my fancy's flight
>   Is ever wi' my Jean.

[1] Directions.

I see her in the dewy flowers,
  I see her sweet and fair:
I hear her in the tunefu' birds,
  I hear her charm the air:
There's not a bonnie flower that springs
  By fountain, shaw,[1] or green,
There's not a bonnie bird that sings,
  But minds me o' my Jean.

Equally tender is the touching memory of Mary Morrison, a tribute written after her early death.

Ye banks and braes and streams around
  The castle o' Montgomery,
Green be your woods, and fair your flowers,
  Your waters never drumlie[2]
There simmer[3] first unfauld her robes,
  And there the langest tarry;
For there I took the last fareweel
  O' my sweet Highland Mary.

How sweetly bloomed the gay green birk[4]
  How rich the hawthorn's blossom,
As underneath their fragrant shade
  I clasped her to my bosom!
The golden hours on angel wings
  Flew o'er me and my dearie;
For dear to me as light and life
  Was my sweet Highland Mary.

Wi' monie a vow and locked embrace
  Our parting was fu' tender;
And, pledging aft to meet again,
  We tore ourselves asunder;
But oh! fell Death's untimely frost,
  That nipped my flower sae early!
Now green's the sod, and cauld's the clay,
  That wraps my Highland Mary!

[1] Grove or wood. [2] Muddy. [3] Summer. [4] Birch.

O pale, pale now, those rosy lips
I aft hae kissed sae fondly!
And closed for aye the sparkling glance
That dwelt on me sae kindly!
And mold'ring now in silent dust,
That heart that lo'ed me dearly!
But still within my bosom's core
Shall live my Highland Mary.

The most famous of Burns's love songs does not seem to have
been written to any particular girl. Like so many of his poems,
it apparently had its origin in a folk tune, but it is hard to tell
where Burns's borrowing ends and where his originality begins.
As the critic James Douglas wrote, "Burns ennobled his larcenies
and glorified his thefts." Whatever may have given Burns the
idea, "My Luve" is a magical transformation of an almost stereotyped figure of speech into simple but imperishable music.

O my luve is like a red, red rose,
That's newly sprung in June:
O my luve is like the melodie,
That's sweetly played in tune.

As fair art thou, my bonnie lass,
So deep in luve am I;
And I will luve thee still, my dear,
Till a' the seas gang dry.

Till a' the seas gang dry, my dear,
And the rocks melt wi' the sun;
And I will luve thee still, my dear,
While the sands o' life shall run.

And fare thee weel, my only luve!
And fare thee weel awhile!
And I will come again, my luve,
Tho' it were ten thousand mile.

It is little wonder that Burns was favored by the girls. He
was an unusually good-looking charmer. His men companions—
and he made friends with men almost as quickly as with women

—were envious of his high color, fine forehead, mobile mouth, and dark eyes that were both playful and passionate. His strong chin and boldly pointed nose emphasized his masculinity. His voice was soft and persuasive; his manner was ingratiating; his wooing was ardent but gentle. No one could resist him. No one tried to.

Burns's love life was a series of easy conquests, but his life as a farmer and husbandman was as unhappy as it was unsuccessful. Attempting to give up farming, he went to Irvine, the distributing center of the flax industry. He started to learn about the growing and dressing of flax, whose fibers were spun into linen and whose seeds were crushed to make linseed oil. The venture was doomed when the workers welcomed the New Year with a rowdy party. During the carousing, said Burns ruefully, "the shop took fire and burned to ashes. I was left, like a true poet, without a sixpence."

Reluctantly he resumed farming. He comforted himself with spells of drinking and love-making, but he suffered much. In a rather theatrical letter, he wrote that he longed to "bid an eternal adieu to all the pains and uneasiness and disquietude of this weary life." A failure as a farmer, a rhymer whom no one took seriously, he was downhearted about the present and afraid of the future.

Poetry saved him. Some of his verses had been circulated in manuscript, and readers began to talk about the plowboy who could turn out a poem as easily as he could turn a furrow. A few friends persuaded him to put some of his verses together and have them printed. As a result, a little book was published by a small press in the town of Kilmarnock and, to Burns's surprise, was a startling success. It seemed that everyone who heard of the book wanted to have it; even day laborers, especially farmhands, scraped up the three shillings it cost. The critics, usually severe with first efforts of unknown writers, praised it unstintedly. One of them was astonished that such work should come from an "unlettered poet"—a misapprehension, for Burns was anything but illiterate. Another spoke of him as "this Heaven-taught plowman," a phrase which stuck. Suddenly, the onetime failure was the moment's fashion. Scotland's capital called him, and he became the darling of Edinburgh society. He could not help but be flattered; his head began to turn. He wrote, half facetiously, "I shall soon be the tenth Worthy and the eighth Wise Man of the world."

Nevertheless, he had misgivings. His good common sense told him that a celebrity of the season was not assured of permanent popularity, that fame was fickle, and that shooting stars burn out quickly. He was aware that "circumstances have raised my fame as a poet to a height which I am certain I have not merits to support." His misgivings were justified. Society soon tired of the country bard whose conversation was so quaint when he was a novelty but which lost its charm when he ceased to be a fad.

Meanwhile his book was selling well. Moreover, he had made an arrangement with a printer-engraver to issue an anthology of Scottish songs, something Burns had much pleasure collecting. With money in his pocket, he returned to the country, married Jean, took over a farm at Ellisland, and got an appointment as Officer of Excise, a kind of inspector whose chief business was to prevent smuggling and illegal sales of liquor.

However, nothing that Burns undertook prospered for long. His tours of inspection led to aimless wandering and even more aimless drinking; while he was away the farm suffered. Ellisland was lovely to look at but unrewarding to plow, plant, tend, and harvest. The poet had chosen it for its beauty; the farmer in him should have known better. It was inevitable that the farm would fail. It took him a long time to realize that he could not keep it up. He then abandoned farming and sold not only all the acreage and livestock at Ellisland but also all the furniture and household goods. He was thirty-two years old when he moved to Dumfries, where he lived the rest of his days, supporting an ever-growing family on the small income he received as an employee of the government.

In spite of adversity, he wrote the madcap "Tam o' Shanter" and some of his most affecting songs: "John Anderson, My Jo," a memorable tribute to married content; "Auld Lang Syne," sung at every convivial gathering; "Oh, wert thou in the cauld blast," written for one who had nursed him; and the pitiful

"Banks o' Doon," composed when he was dispirited and disillusioned even with the beauty of the world.

> Ye flowery banks o' bonnie Doon,
>   How can ye blume sae fair!
> How can ye chant, ye little birds,
>   And I sae fu' o' care!
>
> Thou'll break my heart, thou bonnie bird
>   That sings upon the bough;
> Thou minds me o' the happy days
>   When my fause Luve was true.
>
> Thou'll break my heart, thou bonnie bird
>   That sings beside thy mate;
> For sae I sat, and sae I sang,
>   And wist na[1] o' my fate.
>
> Aft hae I roved by bonnie Doon
>   To see the woodbine twine,
> And ilka bird sang o' its love;
>   And sae did I o' mine.
>
> Wi' lightsome heart I pu'd a rose,
>   Frae aff its thorny tree;
> And my fause luver staw[2] the rose,
>   But left the thorn wi' me.

Most of Burns's poems were written in his native Scots dialect. Sometimes, however, he shaped lyrics in the traditional English manner, such as "Sweet Afton," a perennial classic which begins:

> Flow gently, sweet Afton! among thy green braes,
> Flow gently, I'll sing thee a song in thy praise;
> My Mary's asleep by thy murmuring stream,
> Flow gently, sweet Afton, disturb not her dream.
>
> Thou stock-dove whose echo resounds through the glen,
> Ye wild whistling blackbirds in yon thorny den,
> Thou green-crested lapwing, thy screaming forbear,
> I charge you, disturb not my slumbering fair.

[1] Knew not. [2] Stole.

To relieve his sense of loss, Burns tried to identify himself with local affairs and general politics. He favored both the French and the American Revolution because they promised to give dignity to "honest poverty" and establish a feeling of brotherhood—"a man's a man for 'a that." But his creative days were over. Physically, too, he was nearing the end. A violent attack of rheumatism crippled him badly. His hands shook, his body trembled, and he lost what had always been his salvation in times of trouble: an unfailing zest for life. His wretchedness was increased by the continual pressure of merchants to whom he was in debt. He was forced to write to a cousin begging for a few pounds so that he would not have to die in jail. A week after writing the letter he was stricken with a heart attack and died on July 21, 1796. He was not yet thirty-eight. Four days later, while he was being buried, his last son was born.

A Man Speaking to Men

WILLIAM WORDSWORTH
[1770–1850]

IN HIS QUIET manner William Wordsworth changed the course of English poetry. He changed it in two ways. He showed that the language of ordinary speech was more persuasive, more penetrating, and even more poetic than the stereotyped "poetic diction" with its overdecorated elegance and such phrases as "roseate dawn," "empurpled vistas," "Cimmerian depths," and so on. With the emphasis on an unadorned style, he advocated a return to nature and an appreciation of too often neglected things.

Wordsworth was born at Cockermouth in the lovely Lake District of England, April 7, 1770. His father was an attorney who died when William was thirteen; his mother had died when he was seven. Various uncles took care of him and supervised his education. A thoughtful youth, he was deeply affected by revolutionary ideas he picked up at St. John's College in Cambridge, ideas that were reinforced by two visits to France—one a walking trip while he was still an undergraduate, the other after he had taken his degree. He was intellectually drawn to Republicanism, a free spirit that he praised in a long poem, "The Prelude."

> . . . a spirit was abroad
> Which could not be withstood, that poverty
> . . . would in a little while
> Be found no more.

He fell in love with that spirit and with France because it represented to him the excitement of a new age coming to birth.

> Bliss was it in that dawn to be alive,
> But to be young was very Heaven.

He also fell in love with a French girl, Annette Vallon, who embodied the new revolutionary principles. His love was reciprocated, and Annette bore him a daughter, Ann Caroline. Wordsworth went home in order to collect funds for their support, but he was stopped when war broke out between England and France. Everything was changed; communications were impossible; Wordsworth was unable to return to France or bring mother and child to England.

The separation was made more difficult by his relatives, all of whom, with the exception of his sister Dorothy, disapproved of his convictions as well as his conduct. They would do nothing to aid him. There had been talk of his being trained for the ministry, but the family considered this unthinkable now; one of his uncles refused to let him enter the house. Annette wrote appealing letters. She said that she waited patiently but eagerly for him, that she was spiritually if not legally married to him, and that she looked forward to the time when "my dear William can make the trip to France, give me the title of wife, and I will be consoled."

Circumstances worked against the reunion. The course of the European conflict prevented anything like a happy ending. Shocked by the atrocities which accompanied the Reign of Terror in France and the militarism of his own country, Wordsworth lost faith in revolution and learned to hate war. It was many years before he went back to France, and by then he was married to someone else.

It was on his belated return that Wordsworth took evening

walks along the French seashore with his daughter, who was then ten years old. After one of those walks Wordsworth composed a famous sonnet which illustrates the quality of what he claimed poetry should possess: "the spontaneous overflow of powerful feelings which takes its origin from emotions recollected in tranquillity."

ON THE BEACH AT CALAIS

It is a beauteous evening, calm and free;
The holy time is quiet as a nun
Breathless with adoration; the broad sun
Is sinking down in its tranquillity;
The gentleness of heaven broods o'er the sea.
Listen! the mighty Being is awake,
And doth with his eternal motion make
A sound like thunder—everlastingly.
Dear child! dear girl! that walkest with me here,
If thou appear untouched by solemn thought,
Thy nature is not therefore less divine:
Thou liest in Abraham's bosom all the year,
And worship'st at the Temple's inner shrine,
God being with thee when we know it not.

Wordsworth scarcely looked the way the idealized poet is supposed to look. His nose was unusually long, his forehead flat, his complexion sallow, his mouth lacked firmness. He spoke with a burred country tang. While his sister Dorothy admitted his plainness, she found his face not only thoughtful but lovable, and his smile was so pleasing that there was an "inclination to laughter about the mouth." Dorothy adored her brother, who was a year older than herself, and Wordsworth returned her love. He married Dorothy's best friend, Mary Hutchinson, and Dorothy went along on the honeymoon. When the three of them returned to Dove Cottage at Windermere in the Lake District of England, where Dorothy had made a home for her brother after his unhappy affair in France, Mary's sister Sara was added to the group. The three women took care of the household and, not least, of Wordsworth. Dorothy could not be interested in any other man. William was her only care; she thought of him as her Beloved. In her private *Journals,* which were not published until almost a century after they were written, she confided things hidden from everyone.

> I went and sat with William and walked backwards and forwards in the orchard until dinner time. He read me his poem; I broiled beefsteak. After dinner we made a pillow of my shoulder— I read to him, and my Beloved slept. . . . It is about ten o'clock, a quiet night. The fire flutters and the watch ticks. I hear nothing else save the breathing of my Beloved. . . . Now for my walk. I *will* be busy. I *will* look well and *be* well when he comes back to me. O the darling! . . . My brother was married to Mary Hutchinson. At a little after 8 o'clock I saw them go down the avenue towards the church. William had parted from me upstairs. I kept myself as quiet as I could; but when I saw the two men running up the walk, coming to tell it was over, I could stand it no longer. I threw myself upon the bed, where I lay in stillness, neither hearing nor seeing anything till Sara came upstairs and said, "They are coming." This forced me from the bed where I lay, and I moved, I know not how, straight forward faster than my strength could carry me till I met my beloved William, and fell upon his bosom.

Meanwhile, another person had become an intimate at Dove Cottage. Samuel Taylor Coleridge had been a friend of Wordsworth's for some time, and when they became collaborators as well as fellow-poets, Coleridge was, more than a constant visitor, practically a member of the household. Also in the meantime, Wordsworth had become extremely conservative. He repudiated his early revolutionary ardor, turned against all radical tendencies, and exchanged rebelliousness for respectability. He refused to be drawn into controversies. "I think I can answer for William's caution about expressing political opinions," said Dorothy defensively. "He is very careful, and seems well aware of the dangers of contrary conduct." He took good care that his conduct would remain exemplary.

Wordsworth had been writing ever since he was fourteen; before he was twenty he had determined to devote his life to poetry. He was twenty-eight when, in collaboration with Coleridge, he issued *Lyrical Ballads,* a landmark in English literature. As the title indicates, the poems were in the spirit and sometimes in the pattern of the early anonymous storytelling ballads. They were, accordingly, simple in style, simple in language, and they sought "to give the charm of novelty to things of everyday." Wordsworth revealed the beauty of unaffected straightforwardness and, by so doing, achieved a poet-to-reader intimacy. His plain speech shocked many readers unprepared for such originality; critics abused him for his departure from what had been considered the proper "poetical" way to write poetry. Wordsworth answered them in "observations" prefixed to the second edition of *Lyrical Ballads.* "The poet writes under one restriction only, namely, that of the necessity of giving immediate pleasure to a human being possessed of that information which may be expected from him, not as a lawyer, a physician, a mariner, an astronomer, or a natural philosopher, but as a man. Except this one restriction, there is no object standing between the poet and the image of things."

Wordsworth was unquestionably pleased with the powers of seeing the clear "image of things" and thus putting ordinary sights and experiences into poetry. Poetry, he felt, should transform observation into memorable description. He prided himself that he had "the ability to observe with accuracy things as they are in themselves, and with fidelity to describe them." Actually Dorothy was a more acute observer. It was she who constantly called her brother's attention to small, significant details, to the odd song of a bird or the way a field of daffodils seemed to dance—details which he worked into such a poem as:

I wandered lonely as a cloud
That floats on high o'er vales and hills,
When all at once I saw a crowd,
A host of golden daffodils,
Beside the lake, beneath the trees
Fluttering and dancing in the breeze.

Continuous as the stars that shine
And twinkle on the milky way,
They stretched in never-ending line
Along the margin of a bay:
Ten thousand saw I at a glance
Tossing their heads in sprightly dance.

The waves beside them danced, but they
Out-did the sparkling waves in glee:
A poet could not but be gay
In such a jocund company!
I gazed—and gazed—but little thought
What wealth the show to me had brought.

For oft, when on my couch I lie
In vacant or in pensive mood,
They flash upon that inward eye
Which is the bliss of solitude;
And then my heart with pleasure fills,
And dances with the daffodils.

Although he was called a "nature poet," Wordsworth did not
write only about daffodils, cuckoos, skylarks, and rainbows. He
depicted nature in the broadest sense. He wrote about the
meanest conditions and the poorest creatures, about an old man
gathering leeches in a muddy pond, a solitary Highland girl
reaping corn, a lonely mountain shepherd, a wornout hunts-
man, a stubborn and seemingly stupid child, a forlorn beggar,
an idiot boy. As he expressed it in "Intimations of Immortality":

> Thanks to the human heart by which we live,
> Thanks to its tenderness, its joys and fears,
> To me the meanest flower that blows can give
> Thoughts that do often lie too deep for tears.

Sadness was mixed with pleasure as Wordsworth contemplated the relation of man to nature. He wrote so intimately, so understandingly, because he not only saw but *felt* himself a vital part of it. The scenes he pictured were perceived as much by the senses as by the eyes—landscapes of the mind. In "Lines Written in Early Spring" the poet describes his delight in the "thousand blended notes" heard in the grove in which he is sitting, the primroses blossoming in brilliant tufts, the periwinkle trailing its light blue flowers, the budding twigs spreading their fanlike leaves, and all the birds hopping and playing about him. Yet the poem concludes with the unhappy thought that, while nature brings beauty to everyone, human nature is often far less lovely.

> If this belief from heaven be sent,
> If such be Nature's holy plan,
> Have I not reason to lament
> What man has made of man?

Although Wordsworth spent all except his early years in cautious respectability, he continued to be concerned with "what man has made of man." His troubled reflections are apparent in poem after poem, especially in such sonnets as the ones which begin "The world is too much with us" and "O Friend! I know not which way I must look," addressed to Coleridge, and the agonized appeal to the spirit of Milton.

> Milton, thou shouldst be living at this hour:
> England hath need of thee: she is a fen
> Of stagnant waters: altar, sword, and pen,
> Fireside, the heroic wealth of hall and bower,

Have forfeited their ancient English dower
Of inward happiness. We are selfish men.
Oh! raise us up, return to us again;
And give us manners, virtue, freedom, power.

Thy soul was like a star, and dwelt apart:
Thou hadst a voice whose sound was like the sea:
Pure as the naked heavens, majestic, free,
So didst thou travel on life's common way,
In cheerful godliness; and yet thy heart
The lowliest duties on herself did lay.

As Wordsworth grew older he grew increasingly conservative. The onetime champion of those engaged in the struggle for liberty settled down to a comfortable conformity. He kept silent when Italy tried to free itself from Austrian tyranny; he opposed a free press; he supported an unscrupulous lord against his liberal opponent. He was rewarded with a pension of three hundred pounds and, at seventy-three, was appointed poet laureate.

After his sixties Wordsworth wrote little that is noteworthy. The early fire had died, and he spent much time warming over old poems. He put together a kind of history of the Anglican Church in more than one hundred *Ecclesiastical Sonnets* and worked on *The Excursion,* a heavily philosophic poem of almost nine thousand lines. His eyesight troubled him to such an extent that he had to give up reading. Dorothy had been his constant comfort, but, in his late sixties, her health was impaired, her mind failed, and she died. The death of his daughter Dora added to his grief. Ill though he was, he survived both sister and daughter and did not die until two weeks after his eightieth birthday, April 23, 1850.

As a poet Wordsworth is sometimes too sentimental, too "preachy," and sometimes too prosaic. His weaknesses have been often parodied and his message has been variously interpreted. No one, however, voiced his central thought more quietly yet more convincingly than Wordsworth himself. In "Lines Com-

posed a Few Miles Above Tintern Abbey" he announced his
serene credo when he wrote:

>   . . . I have learned
> To look on Nature, not as in the hour
> Of thoughtless youth, but hearing oftentimes
> The still, sad music of humanity.
>   . . . And I have felt
> A presence that disturbs me with the joy
> Of elevated thoughts; a sense sublime
> Of something far more deeply interfused,
> Whole dwelling is the light of setting suns,
> And the round ocean and the living air,
> And the blue sky, and in the mind of man;
> A motion and a spirit, that impels
> All thinking things, all objects of all thought,
> And rolls through all things. Therefore am I still
> A lover of the meadows and the woods,
> And mountains; and of all that we behold
> From this green earth; of all the mighty world
> Of eye, and ear—both what they half create,
> And what perceive; well pleased to recognize
> In Nature and the language of the sense,
> The anchor of my purest thoughts, the nurse,
> The guide, the guardian of my heart, and soul
> Of all my moral being.

Distracted Dreamer

SAMUEL TAYLOR COLERIDGE
[1772–1834]

"THE POET, described in ideal perfection, brings the whole spirit of man into activity," wrote Samuel Taylor Coleridge. He went on to say that the poet "diffuses a tone and spirit of unity" and accomplishes this by the power of the imagination. This power, continued Coleridge, reveals itself in the balance of opposite or discordant qualities and in the novelty and freshness of old and familiar objects.

This summation of the poet was similar to Wordsworth's (see page 113), but Coleridge surpassed Wordsworth in the power of his imagination and his way of balancing "opposite or discordant qualities." Coleridge was aware of his ability to put profound feeling into poetry. He himself said that "few men put more meaning into words than I."

Coleridge was born October 21, 1772, at Ottery St. Mary in Devonshire, where his father was schoolmaster and vicar. The youngest of ten children, Samuel was intended to be a clergyman like his father and three of his brothers. He studied for eight years at a shabby school as a charity student. He was thoroughly miserable, starved in body as well as mind. He left a record of some of the privations. "Every morning a bit of dry bread and some bad small beer. Every evening a larger piece of bread and cheese . . . Our appetites were damped, never satisfied. My whole being was, with eyes closed to every object of present sense, to fancy myself on Robinson Crusoe's island, finding a mountain of plum-cake, and eating a room for myself, and then eating into the shapes of tables and chairs! What hunger and fancy!"

At nineteen he entered Jesus College in Cambridge. He was not popular with his classmates, one of whom was the gifted and charming Charles Lamb. Few found Coleridge charming. He was not a jolly companion. As the result of carelessness—swimming in his clothes and drying himself off in them—he contracted rheumatic fever, had spells of violent illness, and had to take opium to relieve the pain. It was a habit to which, later, he became addicted. His looks, too, were against him. Though by no means unpleasant, his features were contradictory. "I have the brow of an angel," he once said, "and the mouth of a beast. I cannot breathe through my nose; so my mouth, with thick lips, is almost always open. 'Tis a mere carcass of a face."

A more sympathetic portrayal was offered by Dorothy Wordsworth. Writing to a friend, Dorothy described Coleridge in his mid-twenties this way: "You had a great loss in not seeing Coleridge. He is a wonderful man. . . . At first I thought him very plain, that is, for about three minutes. He is pale and thin, has a wide mouth, thick lips, and not very good teeth, longish loose-growing, half-curling rough black hair. But if you hear him speak for five minutes you think no more of these things. His eye is large and full, not dark but grey. . . . It speaks every emotion of his animated mind; it has more of the 'poet's eye in a fine frenzy rolling' than I ever witnessed."

At Cambridge Coleridge read constantly but studied only intermittently. He was something of a radical in politics and a rebel in discipline. He troubled his instructors. Worse, he lived so carelessly that he got into debt, talked of suicide, and ran off to London. There he suddenly decided to go into the army and enlisted under an absurd alias. Retaining only the initials of his name, he called himself Silas Tomkyn Comberbacke. He was totally unfit for the life of a soldier. He carried out orders poorly, performed his duties reluctantly, and spent much of his time writing verses. His brothers heard of his plight and paid money to have him released. When he returned to Cambridge, the college permitted him to resume his studies, but he did not remain long. Without waiting to take a degree, he left in the middle of a term.

Full of somewhat confused but revolutionary ideas, he wandered to Oxford. Like Wordsworth, Coleridge had been stirred by the French Revolution and had begun formulating extreme democratic principles. He dreamed of an ideal community, a settlement to start with a dozen couples. It was to be in the United States, the country which, after a revolutionary war, had attained complete freedom. The colony was to be situated on the shores of the Susquehanna, a river of which Coleridge knew nothing except that it had a beautiful-sounding name. He invented a title for his scheme. He called it Pantisocracy. The opposite of Aristocracy, it was to be an organization where everyone was socially equal and every man and woman had an equal voice in this utopia.

At Oxford Coleridge met a merchant's son, Robert Southey, who was to become poet laureate. When Coleridge explained his plan, Southey was enthusiastic about the future of a community of kindred spirits. He decided not only to join the organization but to further it by getting added members to purchase a plot of land in what promised to be another Paradise. He persuaded two sisters, Edith and Sara Fricker, to become part of the project. Southey became Coleridge's dear friend and, a little later, his brother-in-law when, at twenty-one, Southey married Edith Fricker, and Coleridge, at twenty-three, married Sara.

Alas, as Burns wrote sadly, "the best laid schemes of mice and men gang aft a-gley." And no schemes so often go "a-gley," or awry or wrong, as utopian ones. The United States was quarreling with England; war threatened; and the dream of a colony of loving unselfish souls keeping house along the lovely Susquehanna had to be abandoned. There was some talk about trying the experiment in Wales, but when bickering broke out, the enthusiasm dwindled and died. Southey complained that Coleridge had not lived up to his part of the contract; Coleridge complained about lack of cooperation. Unhappily the group fell apart. Southey went to Portugal; and Coleridge, with the wife he had married without passion but "from principle," found a cottage in the countryside and went back to poetry.

In the Lake District, Coleridge became an intimate friend of the Wordsworths. He fell platonically in love with Dorothy and worshiped William. The trio seemed to be "three persons with one soul." The two poets collaborated on *Lyrical Ballads,* a milestone in English poetry not only because of the subject matter—realistic—but also because of the treatment—romantic rather than classical. Most of all, *Lyrical Ballads* called attention to the wonders of the world all about us, "an inexhaustible treasure, but for which, in consequence of familiarity, we have eyes that see not, ears that hear not, and hearts that neither feel nor understand." Wordsworth's task was to portray characters and incidents such as might be found in any village; Coleridge's was to write about persons superromantic and even supernatural, "yet procure for these shadows of the imagination a willing suspension of disbelief."

It is difficult to believe that this work was not immediately recognized for the glorious accomplishment we know it is. On the contrary, the critics sneered at it. One of its more important inclusions, "The Rime of the Ancient Mariner," now enshrined in countless collections, was derided because of its "artificiality" and ballad-like "archaisms." Coleridge was discouraged, but he refused to feel defeated.

At this time, he composed part of a poem which became even more famous than "The Rime of the Ancient Mariner." It was "Kubla Khan," a dream poem that he never finished. Coleridge had been reading a book of ancient travels and had fallen asleep after a passage describing a stately palace in "Xamidu." In a heavy slumber, probably induced by the drug which he took to relieve his rheumatic pains, he began composing a poem without (he tells us in the third person) "any sensation or consciousness of effort. On awaking he appeared to himself to have a distant recollection of the whole, and taking his pen, ink, and paper,

instantly and eagerly wrote down the lines that are here pre-
served. At this moment he was unfortunately called out by a
person on business from Porlock and detained by him above
an hour, and on return to his room found, to his no small surprise and mortification, that though he still retained some vague
recollection of the general purport of the vision, yet with the
exception of some eight or ten scattered lines and images, all
the rest had passed away."

We will never know how "Kubla Khan" might have been
completed had the person from Porlock gone about his business
elsewhere. But even in its unfinished form it is a triumph of
the imagination, a fragment whose lines are sheer magic.

KUBLA KHAN

In Xanadu did Kubla Khan
  A stately pleasure-dome decree:
Where Alph, the sacred river, ran
Through caverns measureless to man
  Down to a sunless sea.
So twice five miles of fertile ground
With walls and towers were girdled round:
And here were gardens bright with sinuous rills,
Where blossomed many an incense-bearing tree,
And here were forests ancient as the hills,
Enfolding sunny spots of greenery.

But oh! that deep romantic chasm which slanted
Down the green hill athwart a cedarn cover!
A savage place; as holy and enchanted
As e'er beneath a waning moon was haunted
By woman wailing for her demon-lover!
And from this chasm, with ceaseless turmoil seething,
As if this earth in fast thick pants were breathing,
A mighty fountain momently was forced,
Amid whose swift, half-intermitted burst
Huge fragments vaulted like rebounding hail,
Or chaffy grain beneath the thresher's flail.

And 'mid these dancing rocks at once and ever
It flung up momently the sacred river.
Five miles meandering with a mazy motion
Through wood and dale the sacred river ran,
Then reached the caverns measureless to man,
And sank in tumult to a lifeless ocean:
And 'mid this tumult Kubla heard from far
Ancestral voices prophesying war!

> The shadow of the dome of pleasure
> Floated midway on the waves;
> Where was heard the mingled measure
> From the fountain and the caves.

It was a miracle of rare device,
A sunny pleasure-dome with caves of ice!

> A damsel with a dulcimer
> In a vision once I saw:
> It was an Abyssinian maid,
> And on her dulcimer she played,
> Singing of Mount Abora.
> Could I revive within me
> Her symphony and song,
> To such a deep delight 'twould win me,

That with music loud and long,
I would build that dome in air,
That sunny dome! those caves of ice!
And all who heard should see them there,
And all should cry, Beware! Beware!
His flashing eyes, his floating hair!
Weave a circle round him thrice,
And close your eyes with holy dread,
For he on honey-dew hath fed,
And drunk the milk of Paradise.

Coleridge visited the Wordsworths more and more frequently because of the close communication that had been established. Coleridge's wife considered him a failure, and it was good for

him to be often with people who appreciated his kindling wit
as well as his creativeness. Wordsworth's sister-in-law, Sara
Hutchinson, was fascinated by him, and it was to Sara that he
dictated many of his poems. Yet, although the intellectual atmosphere of the Lake District was all he could desire, the physical
climate was bad for him. The cold mists and continual rains
made his pains worse. As a result he had to depend more and
more on opiates.

Finally he was forced to leave the countryside he had grown
to love. He tried the Mediterranean warmth of Malta, then
Naples, then Rome. His health did not improve, and he returned to England feeling worse than ever. He stayed in London,
but he was not happy there. He and his wife were almost
strangers—there was talk of a separation—and he was sick in
mind as well as body. His relations with the Wordsworths had
become strained when Wordsworth made it plain that he considered Coleridge a burdensome guest.

Coleridge's health and his poetic gift declined simultaneously.
He tried to finish a long poem, "Christabel," which he had
begun years earlier, but little came of it. To support himself
he turned to newspaper writing and, to justify himself, scholarly
essays and technical criticism. He started a magazine, *The
Friend.* It lasted less than a year. He gave a series of lectures
and was gratified to find he could stimulate audiences. He was
even more pleased when two of his children—there were four
of them—wrote poetry which was praised. However, his condition did not improve. He could not recover his creative energy.
"Oh God!" he cried. "It is easy to say 'Why does not Coleridge
do this work or that?' . . . But to write such poetry or such
philosophy as I would wish to write cannot be done amid
distraction and anxiety."

In his mid-forties he found a physician who took care of him
for the last eighteen years of his life. Dr. Gilman and his wife
accompanied the poet wherever he went. Coleridge was never
completely cured, but he was considerably helped. He was able
to write again. He expanded a series of theological papers and
prepared his *Biographia Literaria,* a set of discussions on phi-

losophy and poetry, on the distinction between reason and understanding, and on the difference between mere fancy and imaginative insight. At fifty-two he was elected an Associate at the Royal Society of Literature with a pension of one hundred guineas. There were spells of extreme weakness, but with his doctor's constant help, he survived another decade. He was in his sixty-second year when he died on July 25, 1834.

What sustained Coleridge throughout his many trials were not only the necessary drugs but his friendships and his sense of love. It was a love that extended not only to people but to all creation. Toward the end of that wonderful blend of the natural and the supernatural, "The Rime of the Ancient Mariner," Coleridge pronounced his faith:

> He prayeth best, who loveth best
> All things both great and small;
> For the dear God who loveth us,
> He made and loveth all."

Legendary Lover

GEORGE GORDON, LORD BYRON
[1788–1824]

ONE MAN became the embodiment of the entire Romantic Movement: the late eighteenth- and early nineteenth-century poet George Gordon, Lord Byron. A legendary figure long before he died, he was one of the most fascinating men of his day. Byron had everything in his favor: wealth, great wit, and physical charm—he was often compared to the beautiful Greek Apollo, god of music and poetry. He was not tall, but he gave the impression of height because of the way he held himself. His hair was auburn and slightly curled; his eyes were bright with daring and deviltry; his cheeks were poetically pale; his chin was dimpled; the expression of the mouth was that of a gentle and appealing sadness. He had only one physical defect: he was born lame. This handicap did not prevent him from being irresistible. He was, and still is, a symbol of glamor, the Great Lover.

His nature was tempestuous, an inheritance from "the wild Byrons." His grandfather, an admiral, was a reckless adventurer. His granduncle, known as "the Wicked Lord," had killed a man in duel. His father, "Mad Jack Byron," had run off with another man's wife and, after her divorce, married her. She bore him a daughter, Augusta, and died after he had squandered everything they possessed. To recoup his finances, Captain Byron thereupon married a Scottish heiress, a descendant of King James I, spent all her money, and was forced to leave the country. He died bankrupt in France.

George Gordon, called after his aristocratic mother, was born January 22, 1788. He was the only son of his father's second marriage and suffered a most unhappy childhood. Because of his malformed foot, he was subjected to one unsuccessful operation after another. His mother made things worse. She was a vain and quarrelsome woman with sudden changes of mood. She would overwhelm the child with loving endearments one moment and turn on him the next with cruel teasing. She referred to him as "my little lame brat."

Lord Byron was not born a lord. He came into the title unexpectedly. His granduncle, a baron and an eccentric who liked to tame crickets, had a son and a grandson who were to succeed him. Both of them died when Byron was a child, and after his father's death, Byron, as the sole heir, came into the title. He was only ten when he inherited the family estate, the famous Newstead Abbey. There he was brought up by his mother until he was thirteen, at which time he was sent to Harrow. Like his mother, he was extremely temperamental, sunny one moment, gloomy the next, but he showed flashes of brilliance in any study that interested him, especially literature. He was proud of his accomplishments in writing and reciting, and particularly pleased when his half-sister, Augusta, came to hear him declaim speeches from Shakespeare. Augusta was four years older than he, but Byron felt an affection for her that was to last, sometimes helpfully, sometimes harmfully, throughout his life.

He was a few months more than seventeen when he went from Harrow to Trinity College in Cambridge. He literally lorded it there. He had a large income, and he spent a great part of it on expensive furniture for his rooms at the college, for fencing lessons, for catered food, for a carriage, and for the salary of a groom to wait upon him as well as upon the horses. It did not take him long to get into debt. "Wine and women," he wrote to his lawyer asking for more money, "have dished your humble servant. . . . I am condemned to exist (I cannot say live) in this Crater of Dullness till my lease of infancy expires."

Nevertheless, he managed to amuse himself, make friends, and write poetry. His first volume, *Hours of Idleness,* was published when he was nineteen. He boasted that the book "was praised by reviewers, admired by duchesses, and sold by every bookseller in the metropolis." The facts were otherwise. The reviewers were unkind to the youthful collection. One of them, the critic of *The Edinburgh Review,* was especially scornful about it.

About a year later Byron had his revenge. He published *English Bards and Scottish Reviewers,* a caustic attack on *The Edinburgh Review.* Written in the sharp-edged couplets of Pope, whom Byron greatly admired, it was a brilliant satire not only on the critics but on the poets he disliked: Scott, Southey, Coleridge, and Wordsworth. He made fun of Wordsworth's cult of simplicity, referring to Wordsworth as one

> Who, both by precept and example shows
> That prose is verse, and verse is merely prose.

At twenty-one Byron was entitled to his full inheritance and what should have been a great sum of money. However, he owed so much that there was little left for the extravagant way of living to which he had become accustomed. Nevertheless, he gave a wild party at Newstead Abbey, including a mock ceremony in which he dressed himself as a monk, and caroused with his friends until dawn. His mother berated him for the performance, and Byron retorted angrily. The quarrel grew so bitter that Byron left the place and, with his valet and a friend, sailed for Europe.

He spent two years amusing himself abroad. He rode on horseback through Spain, had a brief romantic affair in Malta, fell in love with Greece, and went to Turkey where, in order to prove that the fabled Leander had done nothing remarkable, he swam the Hellespont without any trouble. His mother died shortly after he returned to England, and, determined to lead a more serious life, Byron sat in the House of Lords and made his first speech, a speech in favor of the workers who were being ruined by the industrialists who were running the country. Shelley said that poets were "the unacknowledged legislators of the world"; Byron determined to be acknowledged both as a politician and poet. He was applauded in the first capacity and, to his own surprise, suddenly acclaimed in the second.

A long poem had been begun during Byron's travels in Europe. It appeared as *Childe Harold's Pilgrimage* when Byron was twenty-four. He woke one morning to find himself famous, the most talked-about writer, the center of gossip, and the darling of society. *Childe Harold's Pilgrimage* was a slightly disguised picture of Byron himself as a disillusioned pleasure-seeker, a worldly-wise observer who was also a passionate if somewhat cynical enjoyer of what the world had to offer. Besides personal associations, the book-length narrative contained several "show pieces," such as the descriptive passages beginning "There was a sound of revelry by night" (a swift glimpse of the battle of Waterloo) and "Roll on, thou deep and dark blue ocean—roll!"

Childe Harold's Pilgrimage was not only the season's favorite novelty but also a spectacular financial success. The first edition was sold out in three days; it became the best-selling volume of poetry in modern times. It attracted readers of every kind, especially women.

Byron had begun by pursuing women; now they pursued him. They were captivated by the celebrity who was also a wonderful showman, by the poet's combination of masculine vigor and almost feminine allure. They would not let him alone. One of them, Lady Caroline Lamb, whose husband was to become Prime Minister, wrote in her diary that Byron was "mad, bad, and dangerous to know," but that "his beautiful pale face is my fate." At first Byron enjoyed her vivacity and welcomed her reckless attachment. But in the end he tried to avoid her. He gave orders that she should not be allowed to enter his house, but she managed to get into his rooms by disguising herself as a page boy.

The last thing Byron wanted to do was to marry any of the women who schemed to be intimate with him. He was concerned with them only when they did not concern themselves with him, and this rarely happened. However, he was piqued by the indifference of Lady Melbourne's niece, Annabella Millbanke, who disliked him and the women who were "absurdly courting him." Byron resolved to make her change her opinion, to charm her and restore his hurt vanity by winning her. He succeeded only too well. After an odd courtship, in which the experienced lover and the inexperienced but intelligent twenty-year-old girl alternately advanced and retreated, Byron and Annabella were married.

It was an unhappy union from the very beginning. Byron may have been an ideal lover, but he was a poor husband. The honeymoon was wretched; the home life was even worse. He not only was callous of his wife's feelings but spoke cruelly and even contemptuously to her. He made her miserable by comparing her unfavorably to his half-sister Augusta. Unlike Wordsworth's dependence on his sister Dorothy and Dorothy's pure and private adoration of her brother, Byron's open love of Augusta, an affection displayed in public, declared in his poems and avowed in his letters, was far from secret. It created a scandal and led to disaster.

The marriage did not last long. Annabella bore Byron a child, but he was unfitted to be a father. He had spells of such depression that Annabella feared he was going insane. Within a year she went back to her parents and she and Byron were legally separated. Byron was blamed by everyone. No longer London's darling, he was banned by the very society that had once idolized him.

Byron was both hurt and outraged. A notorious gossip, he could not stand being gossiped about. He left England never to return, but he left it in style. He traveled in almost royal fashion with three servants and his personal physician, who also kept a diary for Byron's publisher. The carriage in which he journeyed was king-size, carved, gilded, and large enough to accommodate a bed, an arm-chair, and a writing desk. It pleased

Byron to appear in a new role, that of the melancholy exile who showed Europe "the pageant of a bleeding heart." He swept through Belgium and Germany and settled for a while in Geneva, Switzerland. There he became intimate with the poet Shelley, Shelley's wife-to-be, and her stepsister, Claire Clairmont. Claire fell in love with Byron, and though he did not love her, he yielded to her infatuation. He wrote to Augusta, who had heard that he was surrounded by a harem: "As to all those 'mistresses,' Lord help me, I have but one. Don't scold, but what could I do? A foolish girl, in spite of all I could say, came after me . . . and I have had all the plague possible to persuade her to go back again." Claire finally did go back. Shelley and her stepsister took her to England, where she bore Byron's daughter, Allegra.

Relieved but restless, Byron went on to Italy. There he indulged in more romantic affairs and wrote some of his more amorous lyrics. Many of the poems are too facile, the kind of thing a poet can write in his sleep, but the best have lasting value. The first is merely entitled "Stanzas for Music."

> There be none of Beauty's daughters
>   With a magic like thee;
> And like music on the waters
>   Is thy sweet voice to me:
> When, as if its sound were causing
> The charmed Ocean's pausing,
> The waves lie still and gleaming,
> And the lulled winds seem dreaming.
>
> And the midnight moon is weaving
>   Her bright chain o'er the deep,
> Whose breast is gently heaving,
>   As an infant's asleep:
> So the spirit bows before thee,
> To listen and adore thee;
> With a full but soft emotion,
> Like the swell of summer's ocean.

The second poem is more significant. It suggests that Byron was tiring of random dissipations—"the heart must pause to breathe,/And love itself have rest."

> So, we'll go no more a-roving
>   So late into the night,
> Though the heart be still as loving,
>   And the moon be still as bright.
>
> For the sword outwears its sheath,
>   And the soul wears out the breast,
> And the heart must pause to breathe,
>   And love itself have rest.
>
> Though the night was made for loving,
>   And the day returns too soon,
> Yet we'll go no more a-roving
>   By the light of the moon.

Byron resolved to apply himself to his writing, and for a while he led a quiet life. But his wayward impulses got the best —or the worst—of him. "I am," he wrote to his friend, the Irish poet Thomas Moore, "studious in the day, dissolute in the evening." His most passionate as well as his most famous affair was with the twenty-year-old Countess Teresa Guiccioli, who was married to a man forty years her senior and who, more or less with her husband's consent, traveled about with Byron for four years. Byron was wealthier than ever. His poetry was yielding a handsome income; his inheritance increased; he sold Newstead Abbey for about one hundred thousand pounds, almost half a million dollars.

Meanwhile, Byron was writing some of his most brilliant work: "Manfred," "The Prisoner of Chillon," another section of *Childe Harold's Pilgrimage*, and most notably, *Don Juan*.

Don Juan is a witty, half-satirical, half-humorous narrative poem. The central figure is obviously Byron himself; any reader is bound to identify the author with the fascinating, devil-may-care, adventurous hero. Apart from the spirited pace of the poem, which reads like a brilliant improvisation, *Don Juan* is an attack on the society which Byron both enjoyed and exposed. To make his attitude clearer, he began a candid memoir which was to be published after his death. He was in his early thirties, restless as always but no longer eager for adventure. Tired of love affairs, he felt the shadow of death about him. His daughter Allegra had died; his friend Shelley had gone for a pleasure sail and had been drowned. Byron resolved not to waste the rest of his life.

The Greeks were struggling against Turkish tyranny, and Byron became a member of a committee to help their efforts. He did more; he sold his luxurious yacht and chartered a well-equipped one-hundred-and-twenty-ton brig for Greece. He arrived in Cephalonia and went on to Missolonghi, where he put on a uniform and was received by the Greek soldiers with military honors. But he was ill, too ill to go into battle, and he grew more and more dispirited. On January 22, 1824, he wrote a deeply moving poem, "On This Day I Complete My Thirty-Sixth Year." It ends with these stanzas:

> Tread those reviving passions down,
>   Unworthy manhood! Unto thee
> Indifferent should the smile or frown
>   Of beauty be.
>
> If thou regrett'st thy youth, why live?
>   The land of honorable death
> Is here. Up to the field, and give
>   Away thy breath!
>
> Seek out—less often sought than found—
>   A soldier's grave, for thee the best.
> Then look around, and choose thy ground,
>   And take thy rest.

Byron was not to get his wish. He did not die on the battlefield. His health declined rapidly—the exact nature of his illness was never determined—and after being treated for typhus and malaria, he became delirious and died April 19, 1824, a few months after his thirty-sixth birthday.

The self-searching memoir was never published. We will never know what it might have revealed. Byron's good friend, Thomas Moore, brought the manuscript to John Murray, the publisher, with Byron's request that it should be published after his death. Murray called in several gentlemen as to the advisability of making it public. The group included some of Byron's friends who, after reading the manuscript, began by disagreeing and ended by quarreling. It was argued that the character of Lady Byron, who was still living, and that of Byron's half-sister, Augusta, might be damaged by the revelations, and that Byron's own reputation would suffer. Murray solved the problem in the most incredible way—he burned the manuscript. Byron's personal tragedy was climaxed by the death of what was probably his greatest work, a lost literary masterpiece.

Byron's thirst for experience, his emotional energy, his very life may be summed up in one of his own sentences. "The great object," he wrote, "is sensation—to feel that we exist, even in pain." His career sensationally fulfilled his objective.

"O World! O Life! O Time!"

PERCY BYSSHE SHELLEY
[1792–1822]

O world! O life! O time!
On whose last steps I climb,
Trembling at that where I had stood before,
When will return the glory of your prime?
No more—Oh, never more!

THIS UNHAPPY LAMENT was torn from the heart of Percy Bysshe
Shelley. Written in his twenties, it reflects the war of delight
and despair which wracked this impassioned poet through his
brief life.

Shelley was born August 4, 1792, in Horsham, a charming
Sussex village. Son of a wealthy country squire, the first of seven
children, he was petted by his parents and adored by his brothers
and sisters. His was so protected a childhood that he was spoiled
for the rough-and-tumble of growing up. His delicate features,
transparent complexion, sensitive speech, and refined manners
were ridiculed by his schoolmates. They mocked him when they
discovered he knew nothing of such ordinary games as leapfrog
or hopscotch or even marbles. Things grew worse when he went
to Eton. The fellows played practical jokes on the boy who
would not join them in their escapades and mocked him for

spending so much time reading books on science. They called him "Mad Shelley" and drove him almost mad shouting the words through the corridors. He became the jeered-at butt of the school.

At Eton, Shelley lived in a world of fantasy. Besides experimenting with rhyme, he wrote two horror stories full of melodramatic settings and situations, a style known as Gothic; the character of the stories may be guessed from their titles: *Zastrossi* and *St. Irvyne or, The Rosicrucian*. His father paid to have them printed, and Shelley was a published author at sixteen. At eighteen, with the collaboration of one of his sisters, he composed a little volume of imitative and inflated verse entitled *Original Poetry by Victor and Cazire*. These volumes, added to Shelley's other peculiarities, may have surprised his classmates, but it did not endear him to them. A few may have suspected he was a genius; most of them regarded him as a freak.

While he was still at Eton, Shelley fell in love with his cousin, Harriet Grove. He courted her with poems and passionate letters and considered himself betrothed. But Harriet's parents disliked the tone of the letters and what seemed to be Shelley's strange philosophy of life. If there was an engagement, it was broken off; Harriet married someone whom Shelley considered a clod, and the eighteen-year-old Shelley took the rejection bitterly.

He did not remain dejected for long. In his nineteenth year he entered his father's alma mater, University College at Oxford, and although he was not popular, he made the acquaintance of one who was to remain a friend throughout his life, Thomas Jefferson Hogg. Shelley's unconventional opinions, voiced more or less quietly at Eton, were now expressed loudly. He wrote unorthodox articles and startled clergymen by sending them letters with queer signatures. The authorities frowned, but Shelley's odd activities were not treated as anything more serious than youthful eccentricities. However, when Shelley, with the assistance of Hogg, issued a pamphlet entitled *The Necessity of Atheism*, the authorities were outraged. The Master of the college called a meeting, Shelley was summoned, and, when he refused to answer questions, he and Hogg, his fellow-offender, were expelled.

Shelley's father was shocked. He was generally inclined to be tolerant with what he considered his son's erratic behavior, but this was a crisis. Moreover, it indicated a future that might be dangerous. Feeling that Hogg was partly to blame, he offered his son a vacation in Greece if Shelley would separate himself from Hogg. Shelley refused. Then his father tried to persuade the stubborn youth to give up his impractical ideas and go into practical politics. Shelley would not listen to this or any other parental plan. He and Hogg found lodgings in London and lived scantily on what Shelley could borrow from his sisters, until his father, seeing that Shelley was bound to go on his own way, gave him an allowance.

He had not forgotten his first love, Harriet Grove, when he met another Harriet. This was one of his sisters' friends, Harriet Westbrook, the lovely daughter of a retired wine merchant and owner of a coffeehouse. Harriet was only a little over fifteen, but she was already "spoken for" by a clergyman. Shelley was soon seeing her from time to time and writing to her earnestly. When he tried to convert her to his way of thinking, she was alarmed. "You may conceive with what horror I first heard that Percy was an atheist," she wrote to a friend. "At first I did not comprehend the meaning of the word; therefore when it was explained I was truly petrified. I wondered how he could live professing such principles, and solemnly declared that he should never change mine." At the same time she was fascinated and continued to meet him more and more often. She was encouraged to do this by her older sister Eliza, who felt that Harriet would have everything to gain from a marriage with the handsome heir to a large fortune. It was not Shelley's philosophy nor his arguments but his charm that persuaded Harriet. Knowing that their parents would not consent to a marriage, the two eloped to Scotland and were wed in Edinburgh.

This was too much for Shelley's father. It had been hard enough for him to face his wayward son's dismissal from college, but the runaway marriage of this nineteen-year-old boy to the sixteen-year-old daughter of a wine merchant was more than his stern, aristocratic code could accept. He was so outraged that he refused to let the couple in his house. He would not listen to Shelley; he cut off his son's allowance. Only after he learned that the low-class Westbrooks were helping the newly married and improvident pair did he consent to support them. Eliza, who had always acted like a mother to Harriet, came to live with them and managed the household. When Shelley went to Dublin to further the cause of Irish nationalism, he took Harriet with him, and Eliza went along.

His revolutionary ideas found expression in his first major poem, *Queen Mab*. This ambitious nine-part poem of considerably more than two thousand lines was Shelley's protest against all that he found wrong in the world. It was meant to be a document as well as a work of art—Shelley maintained that "the past, the present, and the future are the grand and comprehensive topics of this poem." The range was indeed comprehensive. It included the decline of civilization, the corruption of society, the restriction of all institutions, and the mass terrors of war.

> And priests dare babble of a God of peace,
> Even whilst their hands are red with guiltless blood,
> Murdering the while, uprooting every germ
> Of truth, exterminating, spoiling all,
> Making the earth a slaughter-house.

Queen Mab was denounced not only by the clergy but by the critics. It was continually attacked, so much so that people were curious to see how heretical it could be. As a result, it was reprinted and "pirated" by other publishers. It was considered so bold and blasphemous that, twenty years after Shelley's death, a publisher who included it in Shelley's collected poems was brought into court and charged with circulating a scandalous work.

Shortly after the appearance of *Queen Mab* two things happened that affected Shelley deeply. One was the birth of a daughter, Ianthe; the second was his meeting with Mary. Mary was the daughter of Mary Wollstonecraft, champion of women's rights, and William Godwin, the radical philosopher whom Shelley admired and helped to support. Shelley was immediately drawn to Mary; he felt she sympathized with the demands of his nature much more than did Harriet. On her part, Mary fell unhesitatingly and unscrupulously in love with Shelley. She literally flung herself at him. Harriet claimed that Mary was determined to have him at any cost. "He thought of me and my sufferings and begged her to get the better of a passion as degrading to him as to herself. She then told him if she did she would die." Shelley was in a quandary. By this time he was committed to Mary, but he did not want to desert Harriet. He suggested that the three of them should live together, a proposal that Harriet indignantly rejected. Shelley tried to explain the situation to his friends. He told the novelist Thomas Love Peacock that Harriet could not be his partner for life because she could not feel poetry or understand philosophy; he wrote to Hogg that Mary awakened things in him that Harriet did not even know were there. In short, he made every excuse for what happened next. He and Mary ran away to Europe together.

Their stay in Europe was short. The weather was bad, the food was poor, there was not enough money to pay for rooms in the cheapest inn. In a few weeks they were back. The situation was unpleasant for everyone. Shelley had lost most of his friends; the Godwins turned against the runaways; Harriet was expecting a second child.

Harriet's baby was a boy, Charles Bysshe Shelley, but Shelley did not hear about it until Harriet wrote a letter signed "A Deserted Wife." He was torn by conflicting emotions, emotions made more acute when Mary bore a seven-month infant which died two weeks later. His only relief was financial. His grandfather died and left Shelley a hundred thousand pounds.

Things were somewhat easier now. Shelley and Mary were joined by Mary's stepsister, Mary Jane, who called herself Claire Clairmont, and the three of them kept house near Windsor Park. Mary had another child, a healthy boy, and Shelley had a new flowering of poetry. But the trio was dissatisfied with the English climate and scornful of their neighbors. Shelley saw enemies everywhere; he determined to get away from the society he had condemned and which was contemptuous of him. In his twenty-fourth year, Shelley, Mary, and Claire left England for Switzerland. There, in a suburb of Geneva, they were joined by Byron.

It was a time and place propitious for poetry, especially for love lyrics. Shelley seldom wrote lines more romantically appealing than "Music, When Soft Voices Die," "Love's Philosophy," "The Indian Serenade," and two short poems on the moon.

MUSIC, WHEN SOFT VOICES DIE

Music, when soft voices die,
Vibrates in the memory—
Odors, when sweet violets sicken,
Live within the sense they quicken.

Rose leaves, when the rose is dead,
Are heaped for the belovèd's bed;
And so thy thoughts, when thou art gone,
Love itself shall slumber on.

LOVE'S PHILOSOPHY

The fountains mingle with the river
    And the rivers with the ocean,
The winds of heaven mix for ever
    With a sweet emotion;
Nothing in the world is single;
    All things by a law divine
In one spirit meet and mingle.
    Why not I with thine?

See the mountains kiss high heaven,
    And the waves clasp one another;
No sister flower would be forgiven
    If it disdained its brother;
And the sunlight clasps the earth,
    And the moonbeams kiss the sea—
What are all these kissings worth,
    If thou kiss not me?

THE INDIAN SERENADE

I arise from dreams of thee
In the first sweet sleep of night,
When the winds are breathing low,
And the stars are shining bright
I arise from dreams of thee,
And a spirit in my feet
Hath led me—who knows how?
To thy chamber window, Sweet!

The wandering airs they faint
On the dark, the silent stream—
The champak odors fail
Like sweet thoughts in a dream;
The nightingale's complaint,
It dies upon her heart;
As I must die on thine,
Oh, beloved as thou art!

O lift me from the grass!
I die! I faint! I fail!
Let thy love in kisses rain
On my lips and eyelids pale.
My cheek is cold and white, alas!
My heart beats loud and fast.
Oh! press it to thine own again,
Where it will break at last.

TO THE MOON

Art thou pale for weariness
Of climbing heaven and gazing on the earth,
Wandering companionless
Among the stars that have a different birth,
And ever changing, like a joyless eye
That finds no object worth its constancy?

THE WANING MOON

And like a dying lady, lean and pale,
Who totters forth, wrapped in a gauzy veil,
Out of her chamber, led by the insane
And feeble wanderings of her fading brain,
The moon arose up in the murky East,
A white and shapeless mass.

Shelley and Mary, Byron and Claire Clairmont became in-
separable companions. They took long walks along the lake
front, explored the heights, and in the evenings, sat around the
fireplace entertaining each other with stories they improvised.
Many of the stories were weird, and one of them turned out to
be a model of bizarre fiction. It was Mary who conceived the
tale of the soulless monster and called the work *Frankenstein*.
The pleasant life of the quartet was interrupted by a hurried
return to England, where Claire bore Byron's child. They were
shocked by two catastrophes. Fanny Imlay, daughter of Godwin's first wife, committed suicide. Worse was to follow. Harriet
disappeared. Her body was found floating in a river. She was
scarcely twenty-one when she died, leaving a pathetic letter
imploring Shelley not to take the children from her sister Eliza,
who had watched over them.

It is not known for certain what reaction Shelley had to
Harriet's death. Some accounts have it that he took the tragedy
calmly; others assert that he was tormented with grief and guilt.
Whatever the truth may be, he was now free to marry Mary.
After the wedding, Mary hoped that Shelley's little Charles
and Ianthe would be companions to her own William. Her
hopes were defeated when Shelley applied for custody of the
children. The Westbrooks opposed him; they went to court
and submitted evidence that Shelley had deserted his wife for
another woman, that he had showed no concern for his children,
and that he was unfit to act as their father. The court agreed
with them and refused to let Shelley have custody of Ianthe
and Charles.

Shelley was crushed; he was uncertain what to do or where

to go. When, shortly after his twenty-fifth birthday, Mary presented him with a daughter, Clara Everina, he, Mary, and the children left England. This time they went to Italy. Unhappiness followed them. In Venice little Clara became ill. She had had an attack of dysentery during the trip, and three weeks after her first birthday, she died. The unhappy Shelleys moved to Naples, where the poet wrote "Stanzas Written in Dejection," and, a little later, to Rome. There the heat was so great that William, two and a half years old, succumbed. Mary, who had now lost all three of her children, collapsed. But she did not despair. At the end of the year, in Florence, she had her fourth child, Percy Florence, the only one of her children to live to maturity.

In this period Shelley completed two of his most ambitious works, two plays, "The Cenci" and "Prometheus Unbound." The critics were cruel to both, but Shelley considered these dramas, which caught some of the Elizabethan vigor, his best works. Escaping the raw air and rainy season of Florence, he moved on to Pisa, the last city in which he was to live. Here he was more productive than ever. Among the cherished poems are "To a Skylark" ("Hail to thee, blithe spirit!/Bird thou never wert"), "The Cloud," the sonnet "Ozymandias," "Arethusa," and the superb "Ode to the West Wind" with its exciting opening:

> O wild West Wind, thou breath of Autumn's being
> Thou, from whose unseen presence the leaves dead
> Are driven, like ghosts from an enchanter fleeing . . .

and its inspiring finale:

> Scatter, as from an unextinguished hearth
> Ashes and sparks, my word among mankind!
> Be through my lips to unawakened earth
>
> The trumpet of a prophecy! O Wind,
> If Winter comes, can Spring be far behind?

One of Shelley's rare pieces of inspired prose was written as a reply to an article by his good friend Peacock. Peacock had maintained that the busy world had little place for poetry. Shelley answered with a "Defence of Poetry," a ringing challenge which insisted that it was only the poet who could "lift the veil from the hidden beauties of the world and make familiar objects be as if they were not familiar. . . . Poets," he concluded, "are the unacknowledged legislators of the world."

After defending poetry itself, Shelley came to the defence of a particular poet. Keats had died in Rome of consumption, but Shelley believed he had been killed by criticism. He was convinced that malicious reviews were responsible for the tragic destruction of Keats and his genius. Shelley, too, had suffered from the abuse of anonymous reviewers. "Adonais: an Elegy on the Death of John Keats" was not only Shelley's last major poem but perhaps his greatest effort. Not since Milton's "Lycidas" had a single poem been so passionately conceived and so beautifully wrought. The deathless memorial vibrates with passages as exalted as:

> He is made one with Nature; there is heard
> His voice in all her music, from the moan
> Of thunder, to the song of night's sweet bird;
> He is a presence to be felt and known
> In darkness and in light, from herb and stone,
> Spreading itself where'er that Power may move
> Which has withdrawn his being to its own;
> Which wields the world with never-wearied love,
> Sustains it from beneath, and kindles it above.
>
> The One remains, the many change and pass;
> Heaven's light forever shines, earth's shadows fly;
> Life, like a dome of many-colored glass,
> Stains the white radiance of Eternity,
> Until Death tramples it to fragments.

In the summer of 1822 Shelley rented a cottage on the Gulf of Spezia so that he could indulge his fondness for sailing. He bought a boat, and in early July he and a friend sailed to Leghorn. They were on their way back when their small craft was caught in a sudden squall. The boat capsized and both men were drowned. Their bodies were washed ashore a week later and cremated. Shelley's ashes were placed in the cemetery in Rome where the body of Keats had been buried.

Estimates of Shelley, the man and the poet, differed sharply. His life was a contradiction of cool reason and complete irresponsibility. He seemed to dwell in "some world far from ours/ Where music and moonlight and feeling are one." A lover of mankind, he was, nevertheless, careless of people, especially those who were closest to him. He was belittled for his unrealistic idealism, condemned for his amorality, his self-indulgence, and his self-satisfaction. On the other hand he has been worshiped by many. Mary spoke of herself as "the chosen mate of a celestial spirit." André Maurois has compared Shelley to Shakespeare's sprite Ariel. Matthew Arnold characterized him as "a beautiful and ineffectual angel, beating in the void his luminous wings in vain." Francis Thompson saw him as a childlike seraph dancing "in and out of the gates of heaven, gold-dusty with tumbling among the stars."

The best of Shelley moves us with "unbodied joy," a lyric rapture, a distillation of beauty. He was his own skylark; "from heaven or near it," he poured out his heart "in profuse strains of unpremeditated art."

> Higher still and higher
>   From the earth thou springest
> Like a cloud of fire;
>   The blue deep thou wingest,
> And singing still dost soar, and soaring ever singest.

"Beauty Is Truth, Truth Beauty"

JOHN KEATS
[1795–1821]

> Alas! that all we loved of him should be,
> But for our grief, as if it had not been . . .
> The Pilgrim of Eternity, whose fame
> Over his living head like Heaven is bent,
> An early but enduring monument,
> Came, veiling all the lightnings of his song
> In sorrow . . .

THESE LINES FROM "Adonais," written by Shelley at twenty-nine, are part of the poem mourning John Keats, dead before he was twenty-six. Keats's unfettered range and power are the more remarkable when one considers his limited schooling. The titles of many of his poems, such as "Hyperion," "Endymion," "Hymn to Apollo," "Sonnet to Homer," "Ode to a Grecian Urn," suggest that Keats was a classical student. Byron's *Don Juan* contains a sidelong reference to Keats, the poet who,

> without Greek,
> Contrived to talk about the Gods of late
> Much as they might have been supposed to speak.

Keats was not, as these poems might lead one to believe, the scholarly son of some cultured aristocrat. On the contrary, he

146

was the son of a groom, a man who worked in a livery stable. His father, Thomas Keats, had married the daughter of a livery stable owner, and John, their first child, was born at the Swan and Hoop, an inn connected with the stable, on or about October 29, 1795. A few years after his birth, Keats had two brothers, George and Tom, and a sister, Frances Mary.

John was a handsome child who grew up to be a beautiful youth. His eyes were dark brown, large and soft; his hair was a golden red. An acquaintance remembered that she saw him only twice "but the countenance lives in my mind as one of singular beauty and brightness. It had an expression as if he had been looking upon some glorious sight." Keats's friend Benjamin Bailey said that Keats's face was the face of "the most loveable creature I ever knew." He was small-boned, finely built, but by no means frail. His features were delicate without a trace of effeminacy, for Keats was pugnacious, "ever a fighter." One of his schoolmates recalled his "terrier courage," saying that "his brother George, being considerably taller and stronger, frequently had to hold him down by main force."

Keats had anything but an untroubled childhood. When he was ten years old his father was flung from a horse and died of a fractured skull. Less than three months later, with what seems like indecent haste, his mother married an adventurer somewhat younger than herself. It was an unsuccessful marriage. There was a separation, and the children were cared for by Mrs. John Jennings, their paternal grandmother, whom Keats praised in two of his poems.

The Jenningses were fairly prosperous, and the Keats children lacked for nothing. Conscious of her responsibilities and the fact that she was in her late seventies, Mrs. Jennings appointed a friend, Richard Abbey, a tea merchant, to act as guardian to look after her grandchildren's future. When she died, George was employed as a bookkeeper by Mr. Abbey and John was apprenticed to an apothecary who was also a physician. Young Keats was interested in the uses of pills and potions, but poetry was far more fascinating to him. He could not wait to leave the laboratory for long walks with the somewhat older Cowden

Clarke, son of the headmaster of the school near London which Keats had attended. Clarke was now an instructor at that school, and the two youths talked endlessly about their favorite poets, quoted Shakespeare and Milton to each other, and reveled in the rich romanticism of Spenser's *The Faerie Queene.* "He went through it," wrote Clarke, "like a young horse through a spring meadow—ramping!" Nevertheless, Keats plodded along with his daily work and just before his twentieth birthday went to Guy's Hospital to continue his medical studies.

Incidentally, Keats's varied background is richly illuminated in two modern short stories: E. M. Forster's "Mr. and Mrs. Abbey's Difficulties" and Rudyard Kipling's fictional fantasy "Wireless." The latter story deals largely with the creation of "The Eve of St. Agnes." Before Keats could construct this masterpiece, he had to struggle with anatomy, midwifery, botany, and lectures on materia medica. It was some time before he realized he could never be a doctor, much less what Abbey hoped he would be, a surgeon.

"My last operation was the opening of a man's artery," he said ruefully. "I did it with the utmost nicety but, reflecting on what passed through my mind at the time, my dexterity seemed a miracle, and I never took up the lancet again." He had received a certificate entitling him to be an apothecary, but he knew what he really wanted to be. He was twenty-one when he told Abbey that he did not intend to be a surgeon.

"Not intend to be a surgeon?" exclaimed Keats's guardian. "What *do* you intend to be?"

"I intend to rely on my ability as a poet," said Keats.

"John," said Abbey, "you are either mad or a fool."

Keats had already written a few poems, but most of them were imitations and exercises, nothing to give him assurance that he would someday be ranked among the greatest of English poets. It was Cowden Clarke who caused the first truly Keatsian poem. Keats was living with his brothers in a noisy part of London when Clarke brought him a volume of Homer translated by the Elizabethan dramatist George Chapman. The two

spent hours over the book, excitedly reading the stirring passages to each other. The next morning Keats, who had been
unable to sleep, sent Clarke a sonnet entitled "On First Looking into Chapman's Homer."

> Much have I travelled in the realms of gold,
>   And many goodly states and kingdoms seen;
>   Round many western islands have I been
> Which bards in fealty to Apollo hold.
> Oft of one wide expanse had I been told
>   That deep-browed Homer ruled as his demesne:
>   Yet did I never breathe its pure serene
> Till I heard Chapman speak out loud and bold.
>
> Then felt I like some watcher of the skies
>   When a new planet swims into his ken;
> Or like stout Cortez when with eagle eyes
>   He stared at the Pacific—and all his men
> Looked at each other with a wild surmise—
>   Silent, upon a peak in Darien.

Keats had forgotten that it was Balboa, not Cortez, who had
discovered the Pacific. But, in spite of the error, the dramatic
moment was fixed for all time, and the essence of Keats is
already apparent in such phrases as "pure serene" and "wild
surmise."

The poet had come of age. The critic and versifier Leigh
Hunt, who was to become Keats's close friend and ardent
defender, arranged for Keats's debut in a magazine which Hunt
was editing, and Hunt wrote an article praising the youngest
of the new poets who would "put a spirit of youth in everything." Thus encouraged, Keats gave all his time to a poetry
which should do what he felt poetry was meant to do: "surprise
by a fine excess." He spent hours in the British Museum and
immortalized its treasures in two sonnets and the "Ode on a
Grecian Urn" with its unforgettable beginning and ending:

Thou still unravished bride of quietness,
  Thou foster-child of silence and slow time,
Sylvan historian, who canst thus express
  A flowery tale more sweetly than our rhyme . . .

When old age shall this generation waste,
  Thou shalt remain, in midst of other woe
Than ours, a friend to man, to whom thou say'st,
  "Beauty is truth, truth beauty—that is all
    Ye know on earth, and all ye need to know."

Keats began to move in a literary circle. It was a circle that included, besides Hunt, the painter Benjamin Haydon ("glorious Haydon"), whose huge canvases Keats greatly admired; William Hazlitt, whose critical essays he applauded; and Shelley, of whom he disapproved. Keats was twenty-two when his first book was published. Outside the circle, it attracted little attention. There were practically no sales, and Abbey felt justified in his scorn of poetry as a career for Keats. Several years after Keats's death, Abbey told how the young poet had brought him "a little book which he had got printed. When next we met I said, 'Well, John, I have read your book, and it reminds me of the Quaker's horse—hard to catch and good for nothing when caught.' " When George Keats reproached the publishers for not doing anything to help the sale of his brother's book, they retorted that they were glad to be rid of it and would not care to publish anything more by an author who would only cause them annoyance.

Fortunately Keats found a publisher for his second book and began a long allegory using the framework of the legend of the Greek shepherd beloved by the moon goddess. He wrote to George that *Endymion* would be his test. It would be "a trial of my powers of imagination and chiefly of my invention— by which I must make 4000 lines of one bare circumstance and fill them with poetry. . . . I have heard Hunt ask 'Why endeavor after a long poem?' To which I should answer: Do not the lovers of poetry like to have a little region to wander in where they may pick and choose, and in which the images are so numerous that many are forgotten and found new in a second reading."

The reception of *Endymion* was not merely a disappointment to Keats but a cruel blow. Wordsworth found it "a pretty piece of paganism." Hearing of this curt disposal, Keats rejoined, "Are we to be bullied into a certain philosophy engendered in the whims of an egoist? We hate poetry that has a palpable design upon us, and, if we do not agree, seems to put its hand in its breeches pocket. Poetry should be great and unobtrusive, a thing which enters one's soul."

The indifference shown to his first book had prepared him for condescension toward his second. But he did not expect contempt. The reviewer in *Blackwood's Magazine,* which had been anti-Hunt, attacked Keats as Hunt's latest protégé, jeered at what they called a failure to distinguish between the refined language of Englishmen and the speech of Cockneys, illiterate Londoners. The review made fun of Keats's image-crowded style. "Notwithstanding all this gossamer work, Johnny's affectations are not entirely confined to objects purely ethereal," it went on, and ended with a vulgar thrust: "It is better and wiser to be a starved apothecary than a starved poet. So back to the shop, Mr. John, back to plasters, pills, and ointment boxes."

This was disheartening enough. But *The Quarterly Review* was worse. "We doubt that any man in his senses would put his real name to such a rhapsody," it said. "He is unhappily a disciple of the new school of what has been called Cockney Poetry, which may be defined to consist of the most incongruous ideas in the most uncouth language. . . . If anyone is bold enough to purchase this 'poetic romance' and, so much more patient than ourselves, get beyond the first book and find a meaning, we entreat him to make us acquainted with his success."

It is said that Keats was so devastated by the brutal reviews that he considered abandoning writing and going back, as *Blackwood's* had advised, to "plasters, pills, and ointment boxes." In "Adonais" Shelley implied that the reviewers had inflicted a mortal blow, and Byron, parodying "Who killed Cock Robin," wrote:

"Who killed John Keats?"
"I," said the *Quarterly,*
So savage and tartarly,
" 'Twas one of my feats."

Although deeply wounded by the vicious assaults, Keats was not killed by them. He had other woes, greatly aggravating troubles. His brother George, to whom he had looked for comfort, married and emigrated to Kentucky. His brother Tom died of consumption, the dreaded family illness to which his mother had succumbed and which was to kill George as well as Keats himself. A more insidious disturbance affected him violently just before Tom's death. He fell in love.

After Tom died, Keats moved into a friend's house in Hampstead, then a suburb of London. It was a semi-detached villa; Keats occupied half of it, and a widow and her daughter, Fanny Brawne, lived in the other half. Fanny was a lively eighteen-year-old girl, lighthearted and something of a flirt. In a letter to George, Keats spoke of her as "beautiful and elegant, graceful, silly, fashionable, and strange—we have a little tiff now and then." Keats was concealing the depth of his feelings. He went on to describe Fanny: "She is about my height—with a fine style of countenance of the lengthened sort—she manages to make her hair look very well. . . . Her profile is better than her full face, which indeed is not full but pale; her shape is very graceful and so are her movements." Her light, teasing manner bothered him; he concludes his description by saying, "I was lately forced to make use of the term 'Minx.' " Nevertheless, a few months after the first meeting, he and Fanny became engaged.

It was not a happy engagement. Keats was wildly jealous. He tormented Fanny and himself with passionate protests and frantic letters. When he was not with her, the thought that she might be smiling at someone else drove him into a frenzy. Marriage presented an even more anxious problem. The sums that Abbey doled out to Keats were not enough to support a wife. He must earn money, somehow. He thought of journalism, of returning to doctoring, even, as Abbey suggested, learning hat-making. Desperately, he tore himself away from Fanny in order to make a financial success at writing. Here are some sentences wrenched from his letters: "Knowing well that my life must be passed in fatigue and trouble, I have been endeavoring to wean myself from you. As far as they regard myself, I can despise all events. But I cannot cease to love you. . . . I feel myself at your mercy . . . Tell me you will never be less kind to me than yesterday. You dazzled me. I have had a thousand kisses, for which with my whole soul I thank love—but if you should deny me the thousand and first, 'twould put me to the proof how great a misery I should live through. . . . My love has made me selfish. I cannot exist without you. I am forgetful of every thing but seeing you again. My life seems to stop there—I see no further. I cannot breathe without you."

In a period of feverish intensity Keats wrote some of his greatest poems. It was as if some instinct warned him that he had only two more years to live. He crowded into that short span six odes ranging from the wonderful little "To Autumn" through the poignant "Ode to a Nightingale" to the magnificent "Ode on a Grecian Urn," the gorgeously tapestried "The Eve of St. Agnes," the eerie ballad "La Belle Dame Sans Merci," and such a heart-rending sonnet as:

> When I have fears that I may cease to be
>   Before my pen has gleaned my teeming brain,
> Before high-piled books, in character,
>   Hold like rich garners the full ripened grain;
> When I behold, upon the night's starred face,
>   Huge cloudy symbols of a high romance,
> And think that I may never live to trace
>   Their shadows with the magic hand of chance;
> And when I feel, fair creature of an hour,
>   That I shall never look upon thee more,
> Never have relish in the faery power
>   Of unreflecting love;—then on the shore
> Of the wide world I stand alone, and think
> Till love and fame to nothingness do sink.

And this equally famous poem:

> Bright star, would I were stedfast as thou art—
> Not in lone splendor hung aloft the night,
> And watching, with eternal lids apart,
> Like nature's patient sleepless Eremite,[1]
> The moving waters at their priestlike task
> Of pure ablution round earth's human shores,
> Or gazing on the new soft fallen mask
> Of snow upon the mountains and the moors:
> No—yet still stedfast, still unchangeable.
> Pillowed upon my fair love's ripening breast
> To feel for ever its soft fall and swell,
> Awake for ever in a sweet unrest;
> Still, still to hear her tender-taken breath.
> And so live ever—or else swoon to death.

Keats was not yet twenty-five when the first sign of his fatal illness appeared. He had caught cold during a spell of wet winter weather; his throat grew worse after he had ridden in the rain on top of a bus. He had a severe coughing spell and coughed up blood. He realized at once what that meant. "I know the color of that blood," he said. "It is arterial blood— I cannot be deceived. That drop of blood is my death warrant."

For a while Fanny and Mrs. Brawne took care of him. But his condition needed more than nursing. When the hemorrhages became more frequent, the doctor advised that his only chance of recovery lay in staying for a while somewhere in the warm south. "They talk of my going to Italy," he wrote to Fanny from London. " 'Tis certain I shall never recover if I am to be long separated from you. . . . I see life in nothing but the certainty of your love—convince me of it, my sweetest. If I am not somehow convinced I shall die of agony."

A friend, Joseph Severn, an artist, had won an award which allowed him to go to Italy to paint. Keats went with him. Fanny had volunteered to go along; but Keats, foreseeing possi-

[1] Hermit.

ble deathbed vigils which had depressed him during his term
at Guy's Hospital, would not permit it. The voyage was unusually long and rough; Keats nearly collapsed when they
reached Naples. It was more than a month before he was able
to go to Rome.

Two more months were all that remained for Keats to live.
They were months of an agony that was as much mental as
physical. He wrote to a friend in England: "The persuasion
that I shall see her no more will kill me. . . . I can bear to
die—I cannot bear to leave her. O God! God! Everything I
have in my trunk that reminds me of her goes through me like
a spear. The silk lining she put in my traveling hat scalds my
head! My imagination is horribly vivid about her, I see her—
I hear her! There is nothing in the world of sufficient interest
to divert me from her for a moment."

There was little hope for him now. The pain was so great
that he had to give up the very things which kept him emo-
tionally alive. He could neither read nor write. He would not
open letters, not even those from Fanny. He listened occasionally while Severn played on a rented piano; he was especially
fond of Haydn and Mozart. He pitied his companion who
had to watch him die. "What trouble you have got into for me.
Now you must be firm. It will not last long."

Toward evening on February 23, 1821, he called to Severn.
"Lift me up," he said. "Don't be frightened. Thank God it
has come."

He did not pass away as quietly as he wished. He fought for
breath for seven hours. Then, at midnight, he died in Severn's
arms. He had lived only a few months beyond his twenty-fifth
birthday.

Two days after his death he was buried in the Protestant
Cemetery near the pyramid tomb of Caius Cestius. He had
chosen his own sad epitaph: "Here lies one whose name was
writ in water." At his request there was no name on his tomb.

Beginnings of
American Poetry

WILLIAM CULLEN BRYANT
[1794–1878]

WORDSWORTH SAID that the child is father of the man. William Cullen Bryant, usually called "the father of American poetry," was an established poet when he was little more than a child. He was seventeen when he wrote "Thanatopsis" (literally a meditation on death), one of the most famous American poems. It was not his first work. At nine he composed a poem that was printed in the local paper; at thirteen he wrote a political satire which his father had published and which, a year later, was republished with other of his poems in a pamphlet.

William Cullen Bryant was born November 3, 1794, in Cummington, in the Berkshire hills of Massachusetts, and the lovely landscape of his youth is reflected in practically all his verse. His mother was a descendant of the first settlers who came over from England in the little ship *Mayflower* and landed on the shore of New England in 1620. His father was a country doctor who was also a legislator. Although Bryant lived until his mid-eighties, he was so frail at birth and his head was so abnormally large that he almost died. His father resorted to a desperate method in order to save the child's life. He shrank the infant's hugely swollen head by plunging it every morning in a spring of icy water and continued the treatment for a long time. He

helped to build up the boy's health by making him take long
walks in the woods, no matter what the weather might be. This
was a severe training. Yet it not only made young Bryant well,
but it also made him a naturalist, a lad with a keen eye for
birds, beasts, flowers, and all the varying manifestations of
nature.

His father's library fascinated him—he spent most of the
winter hours buried in books—but when the sun was out he
relished the outdoors with the zest of a true country boy. In an
autobiographical memoir we see him helping the men build a
barn, swinging head down on the ridgepole, joining the apple-
pickers and following them to the cider mill, skipping church
services to go fishing, and doing his best to escape the little
bundle of birch rods which were used for chastising youngsters
and which were as much a part of the household furniture as
the cradle.

It was an age of strict discipline, an age of repression and,
to most children, oppression. "Spare the rod and spoil the child"
was a common motto. It was a time of many duties, many
burdens, and few diversions. But young Bryant was happy with
his outdoor pleasures and his indoor pursuits. He never doubted
that he would be a writer. Moreover, he knew he would be a
writer who could make the most ordinary things in nature
vividly alive.

It is a paradox that his early monologue on death has had a
longer life than most American poems. Wandering in the woods,
Bryant felt a relationship between the solemn poems he had
been reading and the solemnity of the scene: the dark aisles of
trees, the moss-covered trunks of fallen oaks, and the age-old
carpet of dead leaves. Here, in the boy's mind, was a symbol of
man's destiny, his perpetual beginning and ending, his birth,
growth, and final resting place. "Thanatopsis," the poem which
resulted from Bryant's youthful musings, begins serenely:

> To him who in the love of Nature holds
> Communion with her visible forms, she speaks
> A various language. For his gayer hours

> She has a voice of gladness, and a smile
> And eloquence of beauty, and she glides
> Into his darker musings, with a mild
> And healing sympathy that steals away
> Their sharpness ere he is aware.

The poem ends with noble resignation:

> So live, that when thy summons comes to join
> The innumerable caravan, which moves
> To that mysterious realm, where each shall take
> His chamber in the silent halls of death,
> Thou go not, like the quarry-slave at night,
> Scourged to his dungeon; but, sustained and soothed
> By an unfaltering trust, approach thy grave
> Like one who wraps the drapery of his couch
> About him, and lies down to pleasant dreams.

When young Bryant finished the poem, he put it away in his desk. About a year later, Bryant's father found it, copied it, and sent it to *The North American Review*, whose editor had requested contributions from the elder Bryant. Since the poem was in the father's handwriting, the staff believed that the father and not the son was the author. When the poem appeared in the magazine, the editor was told he had been deceived. "No one on this side of the Atlantic is capable of writing such verses," wrote one of the critics. "Certainly not an unknown boy!"

The college Bryant attended was little more than a country school—the faculty consisted of only four instructors—and he had hopes of going to Yale, the eminent college in neighboring Connecticut. But the family suffered financial losses, and the youth was unable to continue further schooling. From seventeen to twenty he studied law in little villages and, at twenty-one, was admitted to practice. At twenty-six he married Frances Fairchild, a country girl, whom he celebrated as "the fairest of the rural maids." For ten years he was a small-town lawyer with fair success. He admired the law in theory, but he despised the way it was often manipulated in practice. Poetry was what he wanted to pursue; poetry was his reason for being.

It was as an American poet—not as an English poet—that he wanted to be known. His brother had written some lines about a skylark, and Bryant teased him about his choice of subject. "Did you ever see or hear a skylark?" said Bryant. "The skylark is an English bird, and an American who has never visited Europe has no right to be in raptures about it."

It was with this thought in mind that Bryant composed his simple, honest, and genuinely native poetry. He wrote about recognizably American birds, flowers, subjects, scenes. He appreciated the dignity of the too-little-respected Indian in such poems as "The Indian Girl's Lament," "An Indian Story," and "An Indian at the Burial Place of His Fathers." He gave a lowly blue flower, the late-blooming fringed gentian, immortality.

Equally famous is Bryant's "To a Waterfowl," a bird of passage that prompted a nature poem which, without obvious preaching, is also a religious communication.

> Whither, midst falling dew,
> While glow the heavens with the last steps of day,
> Far, through their rosy depths, dost thou pursue
> Thy solitary way?
>
> Vainly the fowler's eye
> Might mark thy distant flight to do thee wrong,
> As, darkly seen against the crimson sky,
> Thy figure floats along . . .
>
> There is a Power whose care
> Teaches thy way along that pathless coast—
> The desert and illimitable air—
> Lone wandering, but not lost . . .
>
> He who, from zone to zone,
> Guides through the boundless sky thy certain flight,
> In the long way that I must tread alone,
> Will lead my steps aright.

Bryant's reputation grew so rapidly that at thirty-five he became editor-in-chief of the most important journal in the country. He held the post for half a century, a persevering poet who was also a hardworking journalist. His day began at dawn and ended long after dark. In prose as well as verse he was a fighter for freedom. He championed the rights of labor; he fought for a free press; he spoke up against slavery and predicted its abolition.

Before he was forty Bryant had published five editions of his poems; four more volumes appeared shortly after. At forty he began the first of many travels and was honored wherever he went. When Charles Dickens, the world-renowned English novelist, visited America, his first question on landing was "Where will I find Bryant?" When, in his mid-sixties, Bryant presided at a Lincoln celebration, Lincoln said, "It was worth the journey just to see such a man!" Admirers called him "the first citizen of the Republic."

At seventy Bryant was still young in heart and spirit. He wrote eloquently not only for the Union (the northern states opposed to slavery) but for a reunion of *all* states, for tolerance, understanding, and compassion—for a healing of the wounds made by the worst of wars, a civil war.

At seventy-seven he completed something on which he had labored for a long time: a translation of Homer's *Odyssey*. At eighty he was still vigorous. He started each day with physical exercises and walked for hours at a time. He undertook a revision of the mammoth *Library of Poetry and Song*, composed dozens of hymns, planned new poems, and continued to speak at countless public functions.

In his eighty-fourth year he made an address at the unveiling of a statue in New York's Central Park, a statue of the Italian patriot Giuseppe Mazzini. It was a hot May day, and Bryant stood with bare head throughout the ceremony. Suffering from the full force of the sun, he grew dizzy and fell. He suffered a concussion of the brain, and after remaining unconscious for two weeks, he died, June 12, 1878.

It has been said that in his youth Bryant wrote for his elders, and that in his old age he wrote for children. It is truer to say that, as he matured, Bryant wrote for mankind. He was interested not only in nature but in human nature. Poet and patriot, he left a splendid heritage.

"All's Right with the World!"

ELIZABETH BARRETT BROWNING
[1806–1861]

ROBERT BROWNING
[1812–1889]

THE IMPETUOUS MEETING, elopement, and marriage of Elizabeth Barrett and Robert Browning compose one of the world's great love stories. The lives of many poets were sad, tormented, and tragic. But the years the Brownings spent together were years of calm, creative fulfillment and complete happiness.

Elizabeth Barrett was a prodigy who became something of an unfortunate invalid in her teens. Born March 6, 1806, in the county of Durham, England, she was the most precocious as well as the eldest of eleven children. At eight she read Homer in Greek; at fourteen she wrote an epic, *The Battle of Marathon*, which her father had printed. A year later she was thrown from a pet pony and injured her spine so badly that she had to lie flat on her back for years. She never attended school. Nevertheless, she managed to publish book after book. Her *Essay on Mind* was written at eighteen, her translation of Aeschylus's *Prometheus* in her twenties. She was beginning to recover when a second shock plunged her into a long melancholy: her favorite brother was drowned within sight of the house in which they were living. In her thirties she seemed doomed to a life of illness and withdrawal from the world.

She was not beautiful in the ordinary sense, but she had a

radiance that made up for any lack of conventional prettiness. Mary Russell Mitford, author of *Our Village* and other volumes of country life, pictured her as slight with a delicate figure, "a shower of dark curls falling on each side of a most expressive face; large, tender eyes, richly fringed by dark eyelashes, and a smile like a sunbeam." She was thirty-nine years old when Robert Browning, thirty-three, mounted the stairs to her darkened room and literally swept her off her feet into his arms.

Born May 7, 1812, in a suburb of London, Robert Browning had a mixed ancestry. His paternal grandfather had Creole blood. His mother was part Scottish, part German; her father had been a German-Jewish sailor. Young Browning was educated at home, chiefly by his father, a clerk in the Bank of England. Though not wealthy, Browning's father was comfortably situated. His library held more than six thousand books in various languages, and although his son attended London University, the boy learned whatever he wanted to learn at home. He was as handsome as he was intelligent, and when, at sixteen, he announced he wanted to be a poet, his father was pleased. He saw to it that his son's long poem *Pauline,* a Shelley-like effusion, was published before Robert was twenty-one.

Browning was twenty-two when he made his first European trip. He came back with the idea of a poem that ran to four thousand lines about Paracelsus, the fifteenth-century alchemist who was supposed to have owned a small devil. Browning also wrote a play about the earl of Strafford who was ruined because of his devotion to Charles I. The play was produced by the most eminent actor of the day, but it failed to convince anyone that Browning was a dramatist. Subsequently Browning proved his dramatic gift to an extraordinary degree, but his was a talent for the reader rather than for the theatergoer.

At twenty-six Browning wrote another long (and, to some critics, interminable) poem. This one was the six-thousand-line *Sordello,* a narrative so complicated that few could read it with understanding and fewer still with enjoyment. The poet Tennyson said that there were only two lines in the whole poem that he could follow—the first and last. The first was "Who will, may hear Sordello's story told." The last was "Who would, has heard Sordello's story told." Both lines, said Tennyson, were lies.

Discouraged though he was, Browning did not cease writing; he even insisted on writing for the stage. A few of his plays received production but little praise. However, one, *Pippa Passes,* is still remembered and reprinted. It survives chiefly because of the naïve Pippa's innocent lyrics, especially the song which begins "The year's at the spring."

> The year's at the spring
> And day's at the morn;
> Morning's at seven;
> The hill-side's dew-pearled;
> The lark's on the wing;
> The snail's on the thorn:
> God's in his heaven—
> All's right with the world!

Only a little less popular is another of Pippa's songs. Meditating on God's love and love for all men, she soliloquizes:

> All service ranks the same with God.
> If now, as formerly He trod
> Paradise, His presence fills
> Our earth, each only as God wills
> Can work—God's puppets, best and worst,
> Are we. There is no last nor first.
>
> Say not "a small event!" Why "small?"
> Costs it more pain than this ye call
> A "great event," should come to pass,
> Than that? Untwine me from the mass
> Of deeds which make up life, one deed
> Power shall fall short in, or exceed!

Some of Browning's plays are revived from time to time, but it is in his dramatic monologues—"My Last Duchess," "In a Gondola," "Soliloquy of the Spanish Cloister," "The Pied Piper of Hamelin," "How They Brought the Good News from Ghent to Aix," "Incident of the French Camp," "Saul," "The Glove," "Fra Lippo Lippi," and a dozen others—that Browning is a true dramatist.

The great romance of his life came suddenly. Elizabeth Barrett was an immensely popular poet, and Browning was almost unknown to the general public when he discovered a flattering reference to some of his work in one of her poems. She paid tribute to his sensitivity and his heart "blood-tinctured of a veined humanity." He was abroad when he saw her words, and he wrote to her at once. "I love your verses with all my heart, dear Miss Barrett." He then added, with characteristic impetuosity, "And I love you, too." A correspondence followed, and when he returned to England, a meeting was arranged. Elizabeth Barrett could not rise from her couch—she had resigned herself to being an invalid—but Browning seated himself near her and talked brilliantly and boldly. She was overwhelmed. She was also frightened. She felt she could not dare to fall in love. She was six years older than her admirer; she was ill and would never be well; she wanted to be his dear friend, but she warned him not to speak of love. For a while he acceded to her request, but he never stopped wooing her in one way or another. It was more than a year before she realized that if she were to continue living, she would have to live with him. "I thought I had done with life," she told him later. "And then you came."

There was still a formidable barrier to the lovers' happiness. Elizabeth's father was a tyrannically possessive parent. He wanted his family always around him; he would not permit any of his children to marry, least of all his favorite Elizabeth. When Browning appeared, Barrett became violently jealous; when Browning, abetted by the doctors, suggested that Elizabeth would improve in health by leaving London and staying in some sunny place like Italy, Barrett grew furious. He declared he would move the whole family with him to the country. Although Elizabeth was now forty years old, she was afraid of her father. It took a great deal of persuasion on Browning's part to assure her that she could defy her domineering parent.

Finally she was convinced. One September day she managed to slip out of the house, join Browning at St. Marylebone Church, and marry him there. Accompanied by her little spaniel, Flush, the lovers fled to Paris.

Her father refused to forgive his daughter; he never saw her again. He would not let the other children mention her name; he returned her letters unopened. His attitude was the very thing needed to strengthen Elizabeth's resolve to face life and, if possible, to enjoy it. The result was almost miraculous; she triumphed over every handicap. Suddenly she was no longer an invalid. She was healed, a whole and happy woman. In her forty-fourth year she bore a robust son.

As long as it lasted, the Brownings had a life that was both busy and idyllic. They first settled in Pisa, then moved to Florence, where their home became a meeting place for visitors from all over the world.

One morning in 1847 Elizabeth surprised her husband. He was standing at the window, lost in thought, when he was aware that someone was in the room. It was his wife, who stood in back of him and held him by the shoulder so he could not turn around. Holding him, she shyly pushed a small bundle of papers into his pocket and said, "Read it after I've left. If you don't like it, tear it up." Then she ran to her own room.

Browning seated himself at a table and took out the sheets of paper. On them were written the series of sonnets which have become internationally famous. He was wonder-struck. He knew that his wife was a splendid poet, but he was not prepared for such an overflowing of tenderness. Here was the perfect expression of conjugal love, the unbroken circle of constant bliss, a celebration of the union which is no less ecstatic for being domestic. He rushed to Elizabeth and embraced her, saying, "You have produced a treasure which not only I but all the world will cherish." She murmured that the poems had been written for him alone, but he urged her to let them be published. "I dare not reserve to myself," he said, "the finest sonnets written in any language since Shakespeare's."

The title of the sequence, "Sonnets from the Portuguese," presents something of a puzzle. It has confused many readers

who think the poems are translations from some obscure
original. But the title was personal although it was not meant
to be misleading. It was modest, one more tribute to Elizabeth's
beloved, and it was, to a small extent, an effort at concealment.
But why were the sonnets disguised as "from the Portuguese"?
Why not "Sonnets from the Albanian" or "Sonnets from the
Bosnian," titles which might seem equally appropriate? The
title was one more way of reminding her husband of her abid-
ing love. Because of her olive skin Browning frequently referred
to her teasingly as "my little Portuguese."

Opinions differ concerning the depths and heights of the
sequence, but it is agreed that in these sonnets Elizabeth Barrett
Browning found her most impassioned expression. They combine humility and rapture, an affection which, in spite of daily
contact, is close to idolatry, and an intimacy which breeds not
contempt but content. There may be more profound love poems
in the language, but there are none more quietly poignant.

Here are a favored four:

> Go from me. Yet I feel that I shall stand
> Henceforward in thy shadow. Nevermore
> Alone upon the threshold of my door
> Of individual life, I shall command
> The uses of my soul, nor lift my hand
> Serenely in the sunshine as before,
> Without the sense of that which I forbore, . . .
> Thy touch upon the palm. The widest land
> Doom takes to part us, leaves thy heart in mine
> With pulses that beat double. What I do
> And what I dream include thee, as the wine
> Must taste of its own grapes. And when I sue
> God for myself, he hears that name of thine,
> And sees within my eyes the tears of two.

> If thou must love me, let it be for naught
> Except for love's sake only. Do not say,
> "I love her for her smile—her look—her way
> Of speaking gently—for a trick of thought
> That falls in well with mine, and certes brought

A sense of pleasant ease on such a day"—
For these things in themselves, Belovèd, may
Be changed, or change for thee—and love, so wrought,
May be unwrought so. Neither love me for
Thine own dear pity's wiping my cheeks dry—
A creature might forget to weep, who bore
Thy comfort long, and lose thy love thereby!
But love me for love's sake, that evermore
Thou may'st love on, through love's eternity.

When our two souls stand up erect and strong,
Face to face, silent, drawing nigh and nigher,
Until the lengthening wings break into fire
At either curvèd point,—what bitter wrong
Can the earth do to us, that we should not long
Be here contended? Think. In mounting higher,
The angels would press on us and aspire
To drop some golden orb of perfect song
Into our deep, dear silence. Let us stay
Rather on earth, Belovèd,—where the unfit,
Contrarious moods of men recoil away
And isolate pure spirits, and permit
A place to stand and love in for a day,
With darkness and the death-hour rounding it.

How do I love thee? Let me count the ways,
I love thee to the depth and breadth and height
My soul can reach, when feeling out of sight
For the ends of Being and ideal Grace.
I love thee to the level of every day's
Most quiet need, by sun and candle-light.
I love thee freely, as men strive for right;
I love thee purely, as they turn from praise.
I love thee with the passion put to use
In my old griefs, and with my childhood's faith.
I love thee with a love I seemed to lose
With my lost saints—I love thee with the breath,
Smiles, tears, of all my life!—and, if God choose,
I shall but love thee better after death.

The Brownings enjoyed the rich life of everything Italian. They soon learned the language, adapted legends, and interested themselves not only in art but in politics. "Italy," said Browning, "was my university." The sunny spirit of the land stimulated them and encouraged a warmer poetry than either had previously written. Browning wrote more and more lyrically, yet he never lost his gift for dramatizing. Two of his love poems show how dramatic he could make a situation in the fewest possible lines.

MEETING AT NIGHT

The grey sea and the long black land;
And the yellow half-moon large and low;
And the startled little waves that leap
In fiery ringlets from their sleep,
As I gain the cove with pushing prow,
And quench its speed i' the slushy sand.

Then a mile of warm sea-scented beach;
Three fields to cross till a farm appears;
A tap at the pane, the quick sharp scratch
And blue spurt of a lighted match,
And a voice less loud, thro' its joys and fears,
Than the two hearts beating each to each!

PARTING AT MORNING

Round the cape of a sudden came the sea,
And the sun looked over the mountain's rim:
And straight was the path of gold for him,
And the need of a world of men for me.

In her fifties Elizabeth suffered from a return of her old weakness. She fought against it but was dragged down by a prevailing tiredness. She coughed constantly, and her heart acted erratically. "I am only good for a drag-chain," she wrote. "I feel like a weight around his neck." The coughing spells grew worse; it was evident that she was losing the struggle against tuberculosis. She was sitting in the sun when the end came on

June 30, 1861. She died in her husband's arms—"smiling happily," wrote Browning, "with a face like a girl's, her head against my cheek."

After Elizabeth's death, Browning left Florence. He never returned to the city where he and his wife had spent so many memorable years. He went back to England and settled in London with his son. He continued to create dramatic portraits and penetrating psychological studies of character. *Dramatis Personae* and *The Ring and the Book*, the latter a stupendous and erudite narrative, are two of his largest works. Browning's peculiar fusion of exuberance and scholarliness enabled him to transcribe the multiple aspects of humanity. He gave philosophy a solid substance and turned ideas into persons, persons who, though strange to most of us, are distinct and identifiable. No poet since Shakespeare was a greater depicter of character and the complexity of men's minds. Browning's people are, like human nature itself, curious, often contradictory, but always convincing.

Browning survived his wife by almost thirty years. He never remarried. In his late seventies, for the first time since Elizabeth's death, he revisited Italy. He went there to see his son, who had married an American heiress and who was installed in a Venetian palace. It was in Venice that the aging poet, walking along the Lido one rainy afternoon, caught a severe cold. Bronchitis followed, then a heart attack. While he lay gasping for breath, his son read him a cable from his publisher. His last volume, *Asolando,* which Browning had written in the town of Asolo, had that day been published and the reviews were enthusiastic.

"How gratifying," said Browning. They were his last words. He died December 12, 1889, and was buried on the last day of the year in the Poets' Corner of Westminster Abbey.

The Fireside Bard

HENRY WADSWORTH LONGFELLOW
[1807–1882]

LONGFELLOW has been called "the poet of hearth and home," a characterization which lovingly describes and also limits him. Much of his work was frankly sentimental, and unfortunately, the weakest of it has been popularized through countless high school textbooks. He has been misrepresented as a kindly but tiresome preacher whose sermons are accompanied by the faint tinkle of an old-fashioned music box. His critics have charged him with being a dealer in platitudes, a manufacturer of moral maxims. It is a misleading estimate.

We have begun to revalue Longfellow. Although he sometimes wrote poems which are too pretty and too trite, he gave American poetry new dimensions. He reinterpreted old legends, explored little-known territory, and revealed fresh aspects of the American scene.

He was born February 27, 1807, in the busy seaport town of Portland on the coast of Maine. He never forgot his birthplace. Details are vividly recalled in "My Lost Youth," with its two lines of a Lapland song which act as a kind of chorus and from which Robert Frost took the title of his first book, *A Boy's Will.* Here is one of the verses:

171

> I remember the black wharves and the slips,
>   And the sea-tides tossing free;
> And Spanish sailors with bearded lips,
> And the beauty and mystery of the ships,
>   And the magic of the sea.
>   And the voice of that wayward song
>   Is singing and saying still:
>   "A boy's will is the wind's will
> And the thoughts of youth are long, long thoughts."

Descended from a line of colonial New Englanders, Longfellow's family was eminent in the community. On his mother's
side—the Wadsworth side—Longfellow could trace his ancestry
back to the Pilgrims who had been among the first to venture
into the New World. His father was a prosperous lawyer whose
own father had been a judge. But Longfellow's great-grand-
father had earned his living in a more menial capacity: he had
been a blacksmith. Longfellow's poem "The Village Blacksmith" pictures the worker at his flaming forge with the children
coming home from school, listening to the bellows' roar, and
watching

> . . . the burning sparks that fly
> Like chaff from a threshing-floor.

Alexander Pope wrote remarkably measured verses when he
was still a very young boy. So did Longfellow. A battle poem
was written and published when he was thirteen. He was only
fifteen when he entered Bowdoin College, and by the time he
was seventeen he had determined to be a poet. His father tried
to dissuade him; he urged his son to study law. But Longfellow's mind was made up. "Surely," he informed his father,
"there never was a better opportunity offered for exertion of
literary talent in our country than is now offered. . . . I am
almost confident that if I can rise in the world, it must be by
the exercise of my talent in the wide field of literature."

Even at this early age he could afford to be more than
"almost confident," for his future seemed assured. He was only

eighteen when he was graduated from Bowdoin, but the govern-
ing body of the college immediately established a chair in
modern languages for him. Then, since the youth was hardly
qualified to teach languages he could just manage to read, he
was advised to prepare for the position by studying abroad.

Longfellow was nineteen when, in order to equip himself to
teach, he went to Europe to learn. He remained there three
years, fascinated by France, enchanted by Spain, delighted by
Italy, and in love with Germany. However, he missed the trim
orderliness, the whitewashed tranquillity of New England, its
wineglass elms, its paper-white birches contrasting with dark
evergreens, the cornfields interlaced with great golden pump-
kins. There were, he wrote in a burst of homesickness, "no
orchards by the roadside, no slab fences, no painted cottages
with huge barns and monstrous piles of wood for winter fires."
He never ceased to cherish the lands on the other side of the
Atlantic—he returned to them often—but his roots would not
take hold in any but native soil. He was twenty-two when he
returned to America, married Mary Potter, a judge's daughter
whom he had admired since boyhood, and took up his duties as
professor of modern languages. Although he claimed that he
disliked the academic life, he remained part of it for twenty-
five years.

In most of the textbooks Longfellow is shown as a venerable
sage, a white-bearded patriarch, formidable and forbidding. It
is a pity that the early pictures are so little reproduced, for they
display an unusually attractive man. It is a man with a fine brow
topped with waves of bright brown hair, a mouth that is sensitive but not without humor, and eyes that are both speculative
and sparkling. Longfellow did not wear a beard until he was in
his mid-fifties; he grew it only because his face had been so
badly burned in a tragic fire that he could not shave.

Longfellow was twenty-eight when, after being offered a
professorship at Harvard, he went to Europe for a second visit.
He took his young wife with him; it was to be a combined
pleasure jaunt and an opportunity for further studies in German
and Scandinavian literature. He learned Swedish, took lessons

in Dutch, and, studying Finnish, made the acquaintance of the epic *Kalevala,* whose form and meter were later reflected in his *Hiawatha.* Unfortunately, his wife became ill in Holland, suffered the premature birth of a child, and died in Rotterdam. Longfellow collapsed; he fell into a complete apathy. "I cannot recover my energies in anything. . . . My cherished plans are either abandoned or looked upon as a task which duty requires me to work out."

The sense of duty finally triumphed. He returned to the United States, reminded himself (as he wrote in "A Psalm of Life") that "life is earnest," that "the grave is not its goal," began to teach again, and slowly recovered his energies. In his early thirties he was the honored guest at many entertainments, became a "social spirit," and fell in love with the beautiful eighteen-year-old Frances Appleton, daughter of one of Boston's wealthiest merchants. He idolized her. What is more, he idealized her. He made her the heroine of a semiautobiographical novel. Instead of being pleased, she resented being "unveiled" to the public and, when Longfellow proposed marriage, she rejected him. Nevertheless, he continued to woo the girl who was thirteen years younger than he, and after a five-year courtship, she finally yielded. As a wedding present her father gave the couple the luxurious Craigie House, which once had been George Washington's headquarters in Cambridge, Massachusetts.

The second marriage promised to be even happier than the first. There were five children, including the three daughters, "grave Alice, laughing Allegra, and Edith with golden hair," who are charmingly enshrined in "The Children's Hour." One day, eighteen years after their marriage, husband and wife were sitting with two of the girls. Longfellow was reading and Frances was sealing some envelopes containing locks of the children's hair. A few drops of burning wax fell on her dress, which caught fire. Longfellow rushed to her aid and, throwing a small rug over her, attempted to put out the flames. But she was already so badly burned that she died the next morning. Longfellow himself was so severely burned that, when she was buried three days later, he was unable to attend the funeral. It was the anniversary of their wedding day.

The shock was so great that Longfellow went almost insane. When a well-meaning visitor tried to console him by saying that everyone must learn to bear his cross, Longfellow replied, "Bear the cross, yes. But what if one is stretched upon it!" Although time is supposed to heal all wounds, it did not assuage Longfellow's loss. He refused to speak of it to his friends, but his grief is recorded in several of his poems, especially in "The Cross of Snow," one of the finest sonnets he ever wrote.

> In the long, sleepless watches of the night,
> A gentle face—the face of one long dead—
> Looks at me from the wall, where round its head
> The night-lamp casts a halo of pale light.
> Here in this room she died; and soul more white
> Never through martyrdom of fire was led
> To its repose; nor can in books be read
> The legend of a life more benedight.
>
> There is a mountain in the distant west
> That, sun-defying, in its deep ravines
> Displays a cross of snow upon its side.
> Such is the cross I wear upon my breast
> These eighteen years, through all the changing scenes
> And seasons, changeless since the day she died.

However, since Longfellow had been writing steadily since youth, nothing could stop him for long. His early ballads had been praised by professional critics and favored by the people. Besides a couple of novels, he had published *Evangeline,* a pastoral-narrative poem about a modern Adam and Eve driven from their Paradise, separated, and searching for each other; and *The Song of Hiawatha,* which created a panoramic semi-epic out of Indian mythology. Now he turned to still larger efforts. He translated Dante's *Divine Comedy* and fashioned *Tales of a Wayside Inn,* in which he wove a series of unconnected stories around a central situation. His model was

Chaucer's *The Canterbury Tales,* and the tone was so intimate, the stories were so easily and simply told, that they won his largest audience. The range was great, from the forthright humor of "The Monk of Casal-Maggiore" to the religious revelation of "King Robert of Sicily," the touching legend of "The Birds of Killingworth" and the surging rhythm and patriotic fervor of "Paul Revere's Ride," a true heroic ballad with a forthright beginning:

> Listen, my children, and you shall hear
> Of the midnight ride of Paul Revere,
> On the eighteenth of April in Seventy-five.
> Hardly a man is now alive
> Who remembers that famous day and year.

Longfellow did not deny his debt to Chaucer. He acknowledged it in a sonnet that evokes the spirit of "the poet of the dawn" and ranks with the best of Longfellow's many poems.

> An old man in a lodge within a park;
>   The chamber walls depicted all around
>   With portraitures of huntsman, hawk, and hound,
>   And the hurt deer. He listeneth to the lark,
> Whose song comes with the sunshine through the dark
>   Of painted glass in leaden lattice bound;
>   He listeneth and he laugheth at the sound,
>   Then writeth in a book like any clerk.
>
> He is the poet of the dawn, who wrote
>   The Canterbury Tales, and his old age
>   Made beautiful with song; and as I read
> I hear the crowing cock, I hear the note
>   Of lark and linnet, and from every page
>   Rise odors of ploughed field or flowery mead.

Longfellow made his last trip abroad in his early sixties. He was hailed rapturously everywhere. In Rome he was entertained by the composer Liszt. In England he was given honorary degrees at Oxford and Cambridge. He was invited to Windsor

Castle by Queen Victoria, who noticed how all the servants were impressed and how pleased she was to find that many of his poems were familiar to them. "No other distinguished person has come here that has excited so peculiar an interest," she wrote. "Such poets wear a crown that is imperishable." Twenty-four English publishers had brought out his work. In a single day London bookshops sold ten thousand copies of *The Courtship of Miles Standish,* a long poem based on the history of the Pilgrims who had settled New England. *The Song of Hiawatha* was translated into every modern language and even into Latin.

When Longfellow returned to America he was busier than ever. He completed half a dozen new volumes within a decade. At sixty-five he published *Christus: A Mystery.* It was a three-part work—"The Divine Tragedy," "The Golden Legend," and "The New England Tragedies"—symbolizing the three great ideas and periods of Christianity: Hope, the time of Christ; Faith, the Middle Ages; Charity, the present. At seventy-five he published *In the Harbor,* a significant title, indicating that his journeys were over. It was as if he had foreseen the end, for shortly after the book appeared, he had a seizure and, a few days later, died on March 24, 1882. He was memorialized in marble in Westminster Abbey, the first American to be so honored.

The final estimate of Longfellow's large body of work, over-praised in his day and underrated in ours, is still to be written. It has suffered from changes of fashion, as it suffered from his own facility. He repeated himself; his serenity had a way of slipping into complacency. A skilled craftsman, he wrote in a sometimes wearying succession of meters, shifting manners, unrhymed verses, and stanzas rhymed a dozen different ways. But his virtues should not be overlooked. His gift for transforming European strands into homespun material enabled him to act as a carrier of many cultures, weaving legends and literatures of Germany, Italy, Spain, and Scandinavia into native patterns. Foreign and domestic overtones are captured in such a universal lyric as "The Tide Rises, the Tide Falls."

The tide rises, the tide falls,
The twilight darkens, the curlew calls;
Along the sea-sands damp and brown
The traveler hastens toward the town,
    And the tide rises, the tide falls.

Darkness settles on roofs and walls,
But the sea, the sea in the darkness calls;
The little waves, with their soft, white hands,
Efface the footprints in the sands,
    And the tide rises, the tide falls.

The morning breaks; the steeds in their stalls
Stamp and neigh, as the hostler calls;
The day returns, but nevermore
Returns the traveler to the shore,
    And the tide rises, the tide falls.

Moreover, in his placid way, Longfellow was something of a pioneer. He dug out of native clay the indigenous stuff which went into *The Song of Hiawatha, The Courtship of Miles Standish, Evangeline,* and a score of shorter poems that are now part of the national heritage. Before Walt Whitman called for a poetry which would be recognized as different from poetry produced anywhere else, Longfellow pleaded for a poetry which would be national because it would be natural, rooted in its own earth. "We want a national literature," he asserted, "commensurate with our mountains and rivers, a national epic that shall correspond to the size of the country . . . a national drama in which scope shall be given to our gigantic ideas and to the unparalleled activity of our people."

No poet could have been more unlike the usually gentle Longfellow than the rude, raucous-voiced Walt Whitman, yet Whitman paid the ultimate tribute when he declared, "I should have to think long if I were asked to name the man who had done more, and in more valuable directions, for America." The critical historian Van Wyck Brooks added this comment: "His soul was not an ocean. It was a lake, clear, calm, and cool.

Yet this lake had its depths. Buried cities lay under its surface. One saw towers and domes through the quiet waters, one even seemed to catch the sound of church-bells ringing."

Many different bells were sounded by Longfellow. They rang to rouse as well as to soothe the spirit; they continue to reverberate. He is to be ranked not with the grand old masters nor the bards sublime

> Whose distant footsteps echo
> Through the corridors of Time,

but, as he wrote in "The Day Is Done," with some humbler poet,

> Whose songs gushed from the heart
> As showers from the clouds of summer,
> Or tears from the eyelids start.

Admittedly a fireside poet, a people's poet, Longfellow retains his popularity because of a kindliness which is unaffected and, therefore, winning. He is the poet of the hearth who is also the poet of the heart.

"Weary, Way-worn Wanderer"

EDGAR ALLAN POE
[1809–1849]

WHILE MOST OF his contemporaries were basking in the sunshine of an expanding America, Edgar Allan Poe, journalist, short story writer, and poet, dwelt in the shadows, a forlorn figure, a tragic spirit. The Louisiana Purchase, a vast area of land, was acquired shortly before he was born; southern and midwestern territories were admitted to statehood soon after. The first public railroad was begun and the great Erie Canal completed. But the feeling of amplitude and security could not be shared by one who was, in his own words, a "weary, way-worn wanderer." His sense of isolation was expressed in a poem entitled "Alone," an autobiographical fragment which pronounces his feeling of separation:

> From childhood's hour I have not been
> As others were. I have not seen
> As others saw. I could not bring
> My passions from a common spring.
> From the same source I have not taken
> My sorrow—I could not awaken
> My heart to joy at the same tone—
> And all I loved, I loved alone.

Poe was born January 19, 1809, in Boston, Massachusetts. His parents were roaming actors. His mother, beautiful and frail, was the more talented of the two; his Irish father, quick-tempered and fond of liquor, was as theatrical in private life as on the stage. After many quarrels, David Poe disappeared. He deserted three children and his wife, who died when her second son, Edgar, was three years old. The children were cared for by different families. Edgar was brought up by a wealthy Virginia merchant, John Allan (from whom Poe took his middle name), and Allan's childless wife.

At the age of six Poe was taken by the Allans to England. He remained at school there until he was almost twelve. The presumptive heir of an affluent foster father, he was being educated as a gentleman who would have an important place in the world. Upon his return to America, his education was continued privately and at local schools, but his bright prospects soon faded.

When he was seventeen he entered the University of Virginia, where he indulged himself recklessly. He devoted most of his time to playing, gambling, and drinking. He was not what was known as "a good drinker"; instead of being a pleasant stimulant, a single glass of rum was enough to upset and depress him—and the worse he felt, the more he drank. He ran heavily into debt and, finally, was forced to leave the university; he blamed his foster father for not giving him enough money. It was the first of a series of unpleasantnesses with Allan. Bitter dissension developed when Poe fell in love with a young Richmond girl, Sarah Elmira Royster, and was presumably engaged to her. His letters to her were intercepted; terrible scenes ensued; and three months after being dismissed from the university, Poe left Richmond and ran away to Boston.

He had been writing poems since childhood, and in Boston he spent what money he had managed to save to have printed a thin pamphlet entitled *Tamerlane and Other Poems*. In a brief preface, the author, who was little more than eighteen, said that the greater part of the poems were written when he had barely completed his fourteenth year. Since he was not proud either of his origin or of his foster father, and hoping that his first book might receive the best local response if it were thought to be by a native, he did not use his name. He signed it merely "By a Bostonian." In spite of this and the fact that the book was priced at only twelve and a half cents, it attracted little notice and had practically no sales. Today it is one of the most sought-after of American publications. Twelve copies, most of them imperfect, are known to exist; at a recent sale one of them was sold for more than twenty-five thousand dollars.

Penniless and friendless, not knowing what to do, Poe turned to the army. He enlisted as a private under the name of Edgar A. Perry and was stationed at Fort Independence in Boston Harbor. Although he was promoted to the rank of Sergeant Major, his career in the army lasted less than two years. Allan procured his release and, assuming that the troublesome youth would benefit from a more desirable background as well as better military training, obtained an appointment for him to the Military Academy at West Point. It was a futile hope. Poe shirked discipline, refused to attend chapel, and forgot parades. He was not only stubborn but purposely insubordinate. After six months he was discharged for neglect of duty.

Poe was twenty-two when, after a violent scene with Allan, he was cast out—he had never been legally adopted—and went to New York. He had managed to get a second little volume of poetry (*Al Aaraf, Tamerlane, and Minor Poems*) published in Baltimore, where he had stayed a short while with his aunt, Mrs. Maria Clemm, and her seven-year-old daughter, Virginia. With the book as a kind of card of introduction, he found work in New York as a proofreader and began to write prose.

From this time on Poe's life was a progressively losing battle with poverty, drink, and disease. In a desperate effort to pay his increasing debts, he wrote in a fury of creation and in every possible form: short stories, fantasies, book reviews, philosophical essays, scientific articles, analyses of handwriting, a manual on shells—anything that might keep him alive. A story,

"MS Found in a Bottle," won a fifty-dollar prize, but it was not much help.

Allan died, but although he left money to illegitimate children, Poe was not mentioned in the will. He tried to work on a southern magazine, but he felt desperately isolated; he drank to stave off the thought of suicide. Near starvation, he went to Baltimore and persuaded his aunt to establish a household for him. He obtained a license to marry Virginia, who was now thirteen years old and tubercular. It is more than likely that Poe, at twenty-seven, married his young cousin to make sure Mrs. Clemm would mother both of them.

The next ten years of Poe's life were years of luckless wandering. For a while he lived in Richmond, editing the *Southern Literary Messenger* until he was discharged. In New York he tried unsuccessfully to support his family of three on hack work and routine chores. In Philadelphia, where he issued his fifth volume and contributed to various journals, he obtained a position as editor of a magazine for men, but he was dismissed for negligence. He wrote detective stories, murder mysteries, and other bizarre tales. He collected most of these writings and had them published under the title *Tales of the Grotesque and Arabesque*. A few free copies were the only payment he received for the work.

Meanwhile conditions were steadily deteriorating. Virginia's consumption was much worse; she ruptured a blood vessel and her life was despaired of. She only partially recovered. "At the end of a year," Poe wrote, "the vessel broke again. Then again —and again—and even once again. . . . I became insane, with long intervals of horrible sanity. During these fits I drank, God only knows how often or how much."

When the three moved to New York, Poe could no longer live without artificial stimulants; it was either drink or drugs. With the little money he could borrow and on what his aunt managed to scrape up, he moved the suffering family to Fordham, at that time a village a few miles north of New York. He was so poor that he could not afford to buy stamps to mail his manuscripts or wood to heat the small stove. Since there were not enough bedclothes, Poe's old army coat served as a blanket, and Virginia was kept warm by a ginger-colored cat that slept on her chest. Virginia was a little more than twenty-four when she died and Poe broke down.

Hoping to save himself, he turned to a few people who had shown interest in his work and whom he had helped in their literary careers. There was not much response, but he did become engaged to a widow who wrote poetry, was six years older than he, and had an income of her own. It would have been an advantageous marriage, but Poe could not rid himself of bad habits. When the engagement was broken because he could not stop drinking, he tried to commit suicide. He was saved because his stomach could not stand the overdose of poison.

He felt the presence of death and knew his creative days were over. But there was still a faint chance for him. He went to Richmond to visit his childhood sweetheart, Sarah Elmira Royster, who was now a well-to-do widow, Mrs. Shelton. Poe wooed her quickly and successfully. The date for a marriage was set, and it looked as though Poe's hardships were over. But misfortune, which had never left him, followed wherever he went. On his return north to make preparations for the wedding he stopped off at Baltimore. It is not known exactly what occurred there. A doctor whom Poe had once met received a note saying that Poe was in need of immediate assistance. Poe was found at a polling place. It has been thought that he may have taken a drink in some bar and then, plied with whiskey by political gangsters, had been dragged from place to place as a fraudulent voter until he collapsed. It is also possible that he was recklessly "celebrating" in spite of warnings that the next drinking bout would be his last.

If it was an indulgence, it was indeed his last. Rushed to a hospital, Poe was unable to tell what had happened. For a while he remained unconscious; then, in a state of delirium, he screamed at imaginary specters on the walls. After four days he died, October 7, 1849. His last words were, "God help my poor soul." He was not yet forty-one.

Poe was no sooner dead than his work was alternately hailed

and attacked. It took a long time for Americans to recognize his shattered genius, but he was immediately appreciated abroad. He became a powerful influence in France, especially through Baudelaire, who not only translated Poe but wrote memorably about him. His poems were echoed in the verses of Mallarmé, Rimbaud, Verlaine, and Valéry. Jules Verne was indebted to Poe for his science-fiction fantasies.

Poe was not only a master craftsman of weird tales but also the originator of crime stories and the inventor of the infallible detective. A whole literature of murder mysteries began with "The Gold-Bug" and "The Murders in the Rue Morgue," which introduced a new character in literature: the sleuth who uses his mind like a reasoning machine and solves seemingly insoluble problems by logical deduction. All the famous detectives, from Conan Doyle's Sherlock Holmes to G. K. Chesterton's Father Brown, are the offspring of Poe's Monsieur Dupin. "In fact it is not too much to say," said Howard Haycraft in *Murder for Pleasure,* "that nothing really primary has been added either to the framework of the detective story or to its internals since Poe."

What of the poetry? If much of it is lurid and theatrical, it must be remembered that Poe's life was similarly melodramatic. Moreover, Poe had to devote most of his time to earning a living by all sorts of methods; he was able to be purely a poet for only a few years. Nevertheless, there are not only lines but whole poems which cannot be erased from memory. "To Helen" is one of the most magical lyrics ever composed—magical because its strange music and haunting images take us beyond the meaning. We do not know what is meant by the "Nicean barks of yore," although "the weary, way-worn wanderer" borne to "his own native shore" suggests that Poe might have identified himself with Ulysses. Nor do we understand how Helen's loveliness can have brought him "home" to the ancient world. But the sense is less important than the enchantment of the sounds. Who can ever forget Helen's "hyacinth hair," her "classic face" and "naiad airs," or "the glory that was Greece and the grandeur that was Rome"? The words are like things heard in a vision.

Helen, thy beauty is to me
    Like those Nicean barks of yore,
That gently, o'er a perfumed sea,
    The weary, way-worn wanderer bore
    To his own native shore.

On desperate seas long wont to roam,
    Thy hyacinth hair, thy classic face,
Thy naiad airs have brought me home
    To the glory that was Greece
And the grandeur that was Rome.

Lo! in yon brilliant window-niche
    How statue-like I see thee stand,
    The agate lamp within thy hand!
Ah, Psyche, from the regions which
    Are Holy Land!

"To One in Paradise" is another visionary glimpse. Heart-break and loneliness—two of Poe's main themes—are in this poem, with its particularly romantic, yearning first and last verses. In a less finished form it first appeared in one of Poe's more sensational stories, "The Assignation."

Thou wast that all to me, love,
    For which my soul did pine—
A green isle in the sea, love,
    A fountain and a shrine,
All wreathed with fairy fruits and flowers,
    And all the flowers were mine . . .

And all my days are trances,
    And all my nightly dreams
Are where thy grey eye glances,
    And where thy footstep gleams—
In what ethereal dances,
    By what eternal streams.

Time has softened the shock of some of Poe's spectacular efforts. But we continue to be startled by the dramatic power of "The Raven," with the repetition of its sorrowful "Never-

more"; by the changing sound effects of "The Bells"; by the
varying poems which exemplify Poe's contention that the beauty
of poetry is that it cannot be defined, that an exalted "vagueness" is what should be aimed at—a pleasure which is "the
most pure, the most elevating, and the most intense" because
it is attained by "the contemplation of the beautiful." We sense
this beautiful "vagueness" in such a poem as "The City in the
Sea" (which, with its suggestion of Sodom and Gomorrah—
and perhaps New York—Poe once thought of calling "The City
of Sin"), particularly in its powerful ending:

> The waves have now a redder glow—
> The hours are breathing faint and low—
> And when, amid no earthly moans,
> Down, down that town shall settle hence,
> Hell, rising from a thousand thrones,
> Shall do it reverence.

Equally unearthly is "The Haunted Palace," which Poe implied was a symbol of a mind haunted by phantoms, its "red-
litten windows" indicating the eyes horribly fixed on the evils
of this world. This is its last stanza:

> And travellers, now within that valley,
> Through the red-litten windows see
> Vast forms, that move fantastically
> To a discordant melody,
> While, like a ghastly rapid river,
> Through the pale door
> A hideous throng rush out forever
> And laugh—but smile no more.

In this kind of poetry the outlines waver, the mood shifts
from delight to despair, and the reader moves in a dreamlike
slow motion, "a dream within a dream." It is a poetry of half-
lights and deep shadows, a sad escape. Yet it is real, for it
reflects the world in which Poe lived—a world of glimmering,
ghostly wonder, a world created and inhabited by no one else
but Poe.

"To Strive, to Seek, to Find"

ALFRED, LORD TENNYSON
[1809–1892]

ALFRED TENNYSON was not only the handsomest but also the manliest of poets. Once when he lifted a pony over a fence, an onlooker said, "It's unfair that anyone should be both Hercules and Apollo." Six feet tall, in youth he had the looks attributed to a Greek god: classically carved features, alabaster brow, a helmet of dark hair, a proud but sensitive mouth, the eyes of an eagle. As he grew older he became even more striking. The historian Thomas Carlyle described him as "one of the finest-looking men in the world, with a great shock of rough, dusty-dark hair, bright-laughing hazel eyes, massive aquiline face; most massive yet most delicate. . . . A man solitary and sad, as certain men are, carrying a bit of Chaos about him which he is manufacturing into Cosmos."

Alfred Tennyson was born August 6, 1809, in the village of Somersby in Lincolnshire. His father, a gifted verse-maker, was the rector there, but he was not happy about it. He had not wanted to be a clergyman and, against his will, had been persuaded to enter the Church. There were twelve children, and Alfred, the sixth child and the fourth son, inherited his father's sadness as well as his feeling for poetry. Even as a child he roamed about the countryside and declared that he could hear melancholy voices speaking in the wind. At eight he composed

188

quantities of blank verse and wrote an epic six thousand lines
long; at twelve he analyzed Milton's imposing "Samson Agonistes." At fourteen he wrote two plays and a poem which, revised a few years later, won a prize. At fifteen he was so deeply
affected by the news of Byron's death that he incised a slab of
sandstone with the words "Byron is dead!"

Tennyson was nineteen when, after receiving an early education from his father and publishing a volume of poems in collaboration with his brother Charles, he went to Trinity College,
Cambridge. There he was one of a group of men who were to
become famous: Edward Fitzgerald, translator of the Rubáiyát;
Monckton Milnes, Keats's first biographer; and the brilliant
Arthur Henry Hallam, Tennyson's dearest friend, whose early
death was to be memorialized in what many consider will be
Tennyson's most enduring poem.

Tennyson did not remain in college long enough to take his
degree. He left after three years to go back to the family home,
where his father lay dying. After the death it was said that
Tennyson slept in his father's bed, hoping his father's ghost
would visit him there. Trying to shake off morbid thoughts,
he and Hallam went abroad, and when he returned, Tennyson
resolved to retire to Somerset and peace. Two things disturbed
his tranquillity. *Poems, Chiefly Lyrical,* containing some of his
loveliest verse, received sharply unfavorable reviews, and
Hallam, who had seemed in excellent health, died suddenly and
mysteriously. (It is supposed that death was caused by a blood
clot.) Tennyson suffered a breakdown. Besides having been
Tennyson's "other self," Hallam had been engaged to Tennyson's favorite sister. *In Memoriam: A. H. H.* is a testament of
grief in which Tennyson expressed not only his personal sorrow
but his anguished questioning of life, the conflict between good
and bad, fear and hope, doubt and faith. Here are a few
quatrains from *In Memoriam:*

> Strong Son of God, immortal Love,
>   Whom we, that have not seen thy face,
>   By faith, and faith alone, embrace,
> Believing where we cannot prove,

Thou wilt not leave us in the dust:
  Thou madest man, he knows not why,
  He thinks he was not made to die;
And thou hast made him: thou art just.

Our little systems have their day;
  They have their day and cease to be;
  They are but broken lights of thee,
And thou, O Lord, art more than they.

Oh yet we trust that somehow good
  Will be the final goal of ill,
  To pangs of nature, sins of will,
Defects of doubt, and taints of blood;

That nothing walks with aimless feet;
  That not one life shall be destroyed,
  Or cast as rubbish to the void,
When God hath made the pile complete;

That not a worm is cloven in vain;
  That not a moth with vain desire
  Is shriveled in a fruitless fire,
Or but subserves another's gain.

So runs my dream: but what am I?
  An infant crying in the night:
  An infant crying for the light:
And with no language but a cry.

Ring out, wild bells, to the wild sky,
  The flying cloud, the frosty light:
  The year is dying in the night;
Ring out, wild bells, and let him die.

Ring out the old, ring in the new,
  Ring, happy bells, across the snow:
  The year is going, let him go;
Ring out the false, ring in the true.

Tennyson's brother Charles had married Louisa Sellwood,
and Alfred fell in love with one of the bridesmaids, Louisa's

sister Emily. At twenty-seven he became engaged to her. But the Sellwoods were unwilling that their daughter should marry a poet who had no prospects of a sufficient income. Tennyson's works had little sale; after his father's death there was scarcely enough left to support his mother and sisters. It was not until fourteen years had passed and Tennyson's poems had become popular that the Sellwoods relented. Tennyson was forty-one and his bride was thirty-seven when they were married. He said, "The peace of God came into my life when I wedded her," a statement that was proved by thirty years of undisturbed happiness.

The year of Tennyson's marriage, 1850, was a year of many triumphs. Besides the personal reward after the long waiting, there was public acclaim. With the publication of his new poems Tennyson was recognized as England's most eminent living poet, and on the death of Wordsworth, he was appointed poet laureate. When, a few years later, *The Princess* appeared, readers were captivated by the lyrics which sang their way from one end of the country to another and whose echoes spanned the sea. In spite of changes in poetic fashions, the lines have never lost their melodiousness nor their colorfulness.

Now sleeps the crimson petal, now the white;
Nor waves the cypress in the palace walk;
Nor winks the gold fin in the porphyry font.
The firefly wakens. Waken thou with me.

Now droops the milk-white peacock like a ghost,
And like a ghost she glimmers on to me.

Now lies the Earth all Danaë to the stars,
And all thy heart lies open unto me.

Now slides the silent meteor on, and leaves
A shining furrow, as thy thoughts in me.

Now folds the lily all her sweetness up,
And slips into the bosom of the lake:
So fold thyself, my dearest, thou, and slip
Into my bosom and be lost in me.

*

Ask me no more. The moon may draw the sea;
   The cloud may stoop from heaven and take the shape,
   With fold to fold, of mountain or of cape;
But O too fond, when have I answered thee?
      Ask me no more.

Ask me no more. What answer should I give?
   I love not hollow cheek or faded eye;
   Yet, O my friend, I will not have thee die!
Ask me no more, lest I should bid thee live;
      Ask me no more.

Ask me no more. Thy fate and mine are sealed;
   I strove against the stream and all in vain;
   Let the great river take me to the main.
No more, dear love, for at a touch I yield;
      Ask me no more.

*

Sweet and low, sweet and low,
   Wind of the western sea,
Low, low, breathe and blow,
   Wind of the western sea!
Over the rolling waters go,
Come from the dying moon, and blow,
   Blow him again to me;
While my little one, while my pretty one, sleeps.

Sleep and rest, sleep and rest,
   Father will come to thee soon;
Rest, rest, on mother's breast,
   Father will come to thee soon;
Father will come to his babe in the nest,
Silver sails all out of the west
   Under the silver moon:
Sleep, my little one, sleep, my pretty one, sleep.

One of the most picturesque lyrics in *The Princess* was inspired by a visit to the Irish lakes. There Tennyson had heard

a boatman blowing a horn, and he noted how the echoes resounded, flying wildly among the hills and gradually thinning out, "dying, dying, dying."

> The splendor falls on castle walls
>   And snowy summits old in story:
> The long light shakes across the lakes,
>   And the wild cataract leaps in glory.
> Blow, bugle, blow, set the wild echoes flying,
> Blow, bugle; answer, echoes, dying, dying, dying.
>
> O hark, O hear! how thin and clear,
>   And thinner, clearer, farther going!
> O sweet and far from cliff and scar
>   The horns of Elfland faintly blowing!
> Blow, let us hear the purple glens replying:
> Blow, bugle; answer, echoes, dying, dying, dying.
>
> O love, they die in yon rich sky,
>   They faint on hill or field or river:
> Our echoes roll from soul to soul,
>   And grow for ever and for ever.
> Blow, bugle, blow, set the wild echoes flying,
> And answer, echoes, answer, dying, dying, dying, dying.

Delicate and romantic though most of Tennyson's poetry is, much of it is clearly delineated, graphic as well as graceful. In six lines he captures not only the exact look but the dramatic power of the eagle, and in another six lines suggests the mystery of life, of God and man, in the growth of a wildflower.

THE EAGLE

> He clasps the crag with crooked hands:
> Close to the sun in lonely lands,
> Ringed with the azure world, he stands.
>
> The wrinkled sea beneath him crawls;
> He watches from his mountain walls,
> And like a thunderbolt he falls.

FLOWER IN THE CRANNIED WALL

Flower in the crannied wall,
I pluck you out of the crannies,
I hold you here, root and all, in my hand,
Little flower—but if I could understand
What you are, root and all, and all in all,
I should know what God and man is.

Throughout his life Tennyson maintained his high position. His books continued to stir readers; thousands of each new volume were sold as soon as it appeared. In his mid-seventies Queen Victoria made him a lord. It was said that he was elevated to the peerage because his *Idylls of the King*, set in the legendary days of King Arthur, was a perfect (if prettified) picture of Victorian society.

Honor succeeded honor; at eighty Tennyson was writing with unabated vitality. Invalided by influenza, he never stopped creating. He was reading proof on a new book when he died October 6, 1892, in his eighty-fourth year. His coffin was carried by seven peers, and he was buried next to Browning in Westminster Abbey.

As a poet Tennyson suffered from his own proficiency. He wrote so much and so easily that many of his poems are dulled by their very smoothness; Tennyson could not help being too facile. He yielded too often to sentimentality, to sweetness without strength. But he had not only the vision of the true poet but also the gift of prophecy. Long before the days of the airplane he saw man's conquest of space and the threat of such conquest.

Saw the heavens fill with commerce, argosies of magic
    sails,
Pilots of the purple twilight, dropping down with
    costly bales;
Heard the heavens fill with shouting, and there rained
    a ghastly dew
From the nations' airy navies grappling in the central
    blue.

Yet even here Tennyson envisioned a better future and

> . . . the war-drum throbbed no longer, and the battle
>   flags were furled
> In the Parliament of man, the Federation of the world.

To prophecy Tennyson added purpose. In "Ulysses" he enlarged the myth of the returning hero with a moral significance. He presented the old seafarer as a figure of indomitable courage, a forward-looking adventurer, a seeker after ever-fresh experience—man unwearied and indefatigable.

> . . . My purpose holds
> To sail beyond the sunset, and the baths
> Of all the western stars, until I die.
> It may be that the gulfs will wash us down:
> It may be we shall touch the Happy Isles,
> And see the great Achilles, whom we knew.
> Though much is taken, much abides; and though
> We are not now that strength which in old days
> Moved earth and heaven, that which we are, we are,—
> One equal temper of heroic hearts,
> Made weak by time and fate, but strong in will
> To strive, to seek, to find, and not to yield.

Miracles of Everyday

WALT WHITMAN
[1819–1892]

THE CAREER OF Walt Whitman presents one of the strangest of transformations. Before he became famous as the originator of a new kind of poetry, Whitman was a haphazard, rather ordinary journalist. His *Leaves of Grass* is a monumental book of poems, but it was preceded by a lot of second-rate prose and fourth-rate verse.

Whitman was born May 31, 1819, in his grandfather's house, a small wooden structure in a small community on Long Island, New York. He was named Walter Whitman, Junior, after his father, who was a day laborer. His mother could barely write her own name. There were nine children, none of whom except Walter showed the least talent. Walter was the second son, and the family was not only so large but so poor that there was no chance for the boy to receive any but the rudiments of an education. His schooling was over when he was ten. At eleven he became an errand boy. At twelve he worked as a printer's apprentice. At thirteen he cleaned the press of a Long Island newspaper. At sixteen he supported himself on the few dollars he earned as a typesetter. Between seventeen and twenty the untaught youth managed to teach country schoolboys who knew even less than he did. At twenty he changed his occupation and decided to issue a newspaper. He bought a small, secondhand press and put out a paper in his home town. It lasted a year. He seemed unable to stick to any one thing. For the next six years he worked on various journals until he was editor of the Brooklyn *Eagle*.

The writer was beginning to emerge, although nothing written during this period showed the slightest trace of genius. On the contrary, the editorials were what might have been expected of a young and not too gifted journalist. His attempts at fiction were lamentable. The short stories had such lurid titles as "Death in the School-room," "The Child-Ghost," "One Wild Impulse," "Revenge and Requital." The poetry was worse. It was in rhyme, most of it in dogtrot rhythm, and all of it unbelievably bad. The pieces were sentimental, stilted, and crammed with old-fashioned phrases. "The Playground," for example, begins:

> When painfully athwart my brain
> Dark thoughts come crowding on,
> And sick of worldly hollowness
> My heart feels sad and lone—
>
> Then out upon the green I walk
> Just ere the close of day,
> And swift I ween the sight I view
> Clears all my gloom away. . . .

Whitman did not remain long on the *Eagle*, but during the two years he held the position, he enjoyed himself. He reviewed books of every kind, attended the theater, rode on the tops of omnibuses, and learned the rough language of the drivers, "a strange, natural, and wild-eyed race" who had names like Old Elephant, Balky Bill, and Big Frank. He liked to promenade down Broadway in a frock coat and high hat, swinging a cane and sporting a flower in his buttonhole.

At twenty-nine he was once again without a foreseeable future. Although he had failed as a teacher, printer, journalist, and editor, he refused to think of himself as a failure. He heard of an opening on a newspaper in New Orleans and, with his fifteen-year-old brother, journeyed to Louisiana. He wrote pieces about local subjects, but the owner of the paper did not like the attention which Whitman paid to the so-called "lower classes"—the rivermen, oyster-vendors, stevedores, out-of-work laborers—and four months after leaving the north, he was back in Brooklyn.

Whitman was now free to continue some experiments in writing which he had begun in intervals between one job and another. He had jotted down strange sentences, part poetry, part prose, altogether different from the clumsy verses he had published in the past. On July 4, 1855, when he was thirty-six, Whitman celebrated Independence Day by declaring his own cultural independence. The owners of a little Brooklyn print-shop had allowed him to set up a book of ninety-five pages comprising twelve poems. He called it *Leaves of Grass*. No name appeared on the cover, but the copyright was in the name of Walter Whitman and there was a photograph of the author. It showed a short-bearded man in a careless pose, one hand in a pocket, the other on his hip. The fine tailored coat which he used to wear had been exchanged for a coarse workman's shirt open at the neck, revealing a flannel undershirt. The trousers were also those of a worker; a felt hat was slanted across his forehead.

With the change of garb, there was also a change of name. Walter became Walt, who described himself as "an American, one of the roughs." He was proud of his little book, never imagining that there would be many editions of it and that the ninety-five pages would grow to more than four hundred. He wanted it to be a democratic document, and he had called it after "the democratic herbage," the common grass which grows "wherever the land is."

The book received few reviews. Some were patronizing, but most were unpleasant. Several of the criticisms were abusive. A Boston paper found the book "an impertinence towards the English language and an affront upon the morality of respectable people." The London *Critic* concluded that the author was "as unacquainted with art as a hog is with mathematics."

The first note of approval came from traditionally puritanical New England. It came from the poet and sage Ralph Waldo Emerson. Without reservation the famous Emerson wrote to the then unknown poet as though he were writing to an established artist. He wrote:

> Dear Sir:—I am not blind to the worth of the wonderful gift of *Leaves of Grass*. I find it the most extraordinary piece of wit and wisdom that America has yet contributed. I am very happy in reading it, as great power makes us happy. . . . I give you joy of your free and brave thought. I have great joy of it. I find incomparable things said incomparably well, as they must be. I find the courage of treatment which so delights me, and which only large perception can inspire. I greet you at the beginning of a great career. . . .

Whitman had reason to be grateful to Emerson. He had been influenced by the largeness of Emerson's mind and excited by his philosophy. He acknowledged it pungently: "I was simmering, simmering. Emerson brought me to a boil." Whitman's preoccupation with American (as distinguished from English) literature had also been "brought to a boil" by Emerson. In his essay *The American Scholar,* Emerson had spoken up for a native American kind of writing, a culture without foreign influences: "We have listened too long to the courtly muses of Europe. The spirit of the American free man is suspected to be timid, imitative, tame. . . . Not so, brothers and friends—please God, ours shall not be so. We will walk on our own feet; we will work with our own hands; we will speak with our own minds."

Whitman echoed this sentiment in his "Song of the Exposition" with these lines:

> Come, Muse, migrate from Greece and Ionia,
> Cross out, please, those immensely overpaid accounts . . .

Placard "Removed" and "To Let" on the rocks of your
    snowy Parnassus . . .
For know a better, fresher, busier sphere, a wide, un-
    tried domain awaits, demands you!

Whitman enlarged on this theme. He extended it in many
ways, with American subject matter, American occupations, and
American speech.

I hear America singing, the varied carols I hear,
Those of mechanics, each one singing his as it should
    be, blithe and strong,
The carpenter singing his as he measures his plank or
    beam,
The mason singing his as he makes ready for work, or
    leaves off work,
The boatman singing what belongs to him in his boat,
    the deckhand singing on the steamboat deck.
The shoemaker singing as he sits on his bench, the
    hatter singing as he stands,
The wood-cutter's song, the plowboy's on his way in
    the morning, or at noon intermission or at
    sundown,
The delicious singing of the mother, or of the young
    wife at work, or of the girl sewing or washing.
Each singing what belongs to him or her and to none
    else . . .
Singing with open mouths their strong melodious
    songs.

Whitman was exuberant. He glorified the things that are all
about us; he made them wonderful, miracles of everyday. He
found marvels in what had always seemed commonplace.

The commonplace I sing.
How cheap is health! how cheap nobility! . . .
The open air I sing, freedom, toleration . . .
The common day and night—the common earth and
    waters,

Your farm—your work, trade, occupation.
The democratic wisdom underneath, like solid ground
    for all.

He saw that the large and the small, the immense and the minute, were part of a universal design and that each was equally important. Like Blake, who saw a world in a grain of sand, Whitman declared:

I believe a leaf of grass is no less than the journeywork
    of the stars . . .
And the running blackberry would adorn the parlors
    of heaven,
And the narrowest hinge in my hand puts to scorn all
    machinery,
And the cow crunching with depressed head surpasses
    any statue,
And a mouse is miracle enough to stagger sextillions
    of infidels!

No American poet before Whitman had expressed such a vision in such homely images. The phrase "the parlors of heaven" transformed the traditional "pearly gates" into a comfortable New World sitting room. He introduced into poetry the seemingly unpoetic concept of machinery and made us look at the domestic cow with the eyes of a sculptor.

Whitman was forty-two when the War Between the States began. He did not enlist in the army because he considered himself too old and also because his religious convictions forbade him to take up arms against his fellowmen. His brother George was in a hospital camp, and after a painful visit, Whitman became a male nurse, a comforter and caretaker of the wounded. No task was too menial or ugly for him. He washed the bodies of the afflicted, he carried bedpans, he dressed hideous wounds. He did more. When the soldiers started to recover, he wrote letters for them, read to them, brought books, apples, and sugar to sweeten their stale coffee. Mostly he gave himself.

The new experiences gave him and his poetry added strength.

It vibrated with comradely love. A new series, "Drum Taps," quivered with deeply moving intensity. His poem on the death of the martyred President Abraham Lincoln is one of the noblest elegies in the English language. It begins:

> When lilacs last in the dooryard bloomed
> And the great star early drooped in the western sky in
>   the night,
> I mourned, and yet shall mourn with ever-returning
>   spring.
>
> Ever-returning spring, trinity sure to me you bring,
> Lilac blooming perennial and drooping star in the west,
> And thought of him I love.
>
> O powerful western fallen star!
> O shades of night—O moody, tearful night!
> O great star disappear'd—O the black murk that hides
>   the star!
> O cruel hands that hold me powerless—O helpless soul
>   of me!
> O harsh surrounding cloud that will not free my soul.
>
> In the dooryard fronting an old farm-house near the
>   whitewashed palings,
> Stands the lilac-bush tall-growing with heart-shaped
>   leaves of rich green,
> With many a pointed blossom rising delicate, with the
>   perfume strong I love,
> With every leaf a miracle—and from this bush in the
>   dooryard,
> With delicate-colored blossoms and heart-shaped leaves
>   of rich green,
> A sprig with its flower I break.

After the war Whitman was lonely and ill. He had contracted something he thought was blood poisoning during the time he served as a wound-dresser. At fifty-four he went to Camden, New Jersey, where his mother was living with his brother

George. He adored his mother, and when she died a few days after his arrival, Whitman collapsed. Two years after her death he still mourned her brokenheartedly: "I occupy myself still enveloped in thoughts of her, the most perfect and magnetic character, the rarest combination of practical, moral, and spiritual, and the least selfish, of all I have ever known—and by me, O so much the most deeply loved." He remained in Camden until his own death.

Meanwhile, his reputation had spread not only throughout America but across the Atlantic. He was hailed by English critics and poets, notably Tennyson, Rossetti, Wilde, and Swinburne. Nevertheless, he was poor. The sale of the revised and expanded *Leaves of Grass* yielded little money. He had to live in a dingy set of rooms near a fertilizer factory that sent out nauseous fumes during the day and trains that shrieked by at night. It is said that he was in such poverty that he had to peddle his books around town. Friends helped him with contributions from time to time; the philanthropist Andrew Carnegie sent a check for three hundred and fifty dollars, saying: "Whitman is the great poet of democracy so far."

In his sixty-ninth year Whitman suffered a renewal of the illness which had affected him earlier. He rallied and recovered, but he had difficulty getting about. Somehow, he was able to attend a celebration in honor of his seventieth birthday, but after that he did not appear in public. He was almost seventy-three when he contracted pneumonia and died March 26, 1892.

Seldom has the glory of the commonplace been so symbolized in a single poem as in the lines which Whitman wrote in his mid-thirties and called "Miracles." Here is a part of it:

> Why, who makes much of a miracle?
> As to me, I know of nothing but miracles . . .
> To me every hour of the light and dark is a miracle,
> Every cubic inch of space is a miracle . . .
> To me the sea is a continual miracle:
> The fishes that swim—the rocks—the motion of the
>   waves—the ships with men in them—
> What stranger miracles are there?

The concept of Whitman's major work may be summed up in his simple and direct appeal to the reader:

> Camerado! This is no book.
> Who touches this touches a man.

To this might be added: "Who touches this man, touches mankind."

"The Soul Selects
Her Own Society"

EMILY DICKINSON
[1830–1886]

A WOMAN, an abnormally timid woman, was, with the exception of Walt Whitman, America's greatest poet. She was Emily Dickinson, and she was Walt Whitman's opposite in every way. The history of literature offers few greater contrasts than that presented by these two major poets born within a few years of each other. They and their creations explored the far reaches of American poetry and expressed the extremes of personality. Curiously enough, neither read the other's work.

Where Whitman was immense, earthy, exulting in his "barbaric yawp" shouted over the rooftops of the world, Emily Dickinson was spare, refined (one might almost say distilled), and quiet to the point of a suggestive silence. Whitman rejected formalism of any kind; he erupted in poems that discarded rhyme and, rolling in tidal rhythms, disdained anything resembling strict measure. Contrariwise, Emily Dickinson accepted the tradition of formal verse but, in stanzas rarely more than four lines long, made that form her own. Whitman's utterance was loose, diffuse, rambling, and rhapsodic; Emily Dickinson's was concise, sharply pointed, and because of its precise self-discipline, unerring in impact. Whitman never ceased to talk and write about his aims, his career, and his ever-growing work: "One's self I sing" seems to have been his motto. Emily Dickinson despised not only publicity but publication. She composed countless poems, yet only seven were printed during her lifetime and these appeared without her consent. "Publication is the auction of the mind," she wrote scornfully. Whitman was a man-about-town, lover of crowds, "one of the roughs"; Emily Dickinson was a recluse, a recluse who, in the depths of her quiet soul, was also something of a rebel. Whitman enjoyed the hurly-burly of life; he was everybody's friend, a public figure, a celebrated "somebody." Emily Dickinson shunned the world's notice; she wrote:

> I'm nobody! Who are you?
> Are you nobody, too?
> Then there's a pair of us—don't tell!
> They'd banish us, you know.
>
> How dreary to be somebody!
> How public, like a frog
> To tell your name the livelong day
> To an admiring bog!

Most of Emily Dickinson's life was spent in the house in which she was born December 10, 1830, in Amherst, Massachusetts. Except for a few short trips in early womanhood, she never left it. She had, it seemed, little need of the outside world; her room was her universe. "To live is so startling," she wrote to a correspondent, "it leaves but little time for other occupations." She was socially and intellectually equipped to enter the society of her day, but she chose to stay outside and look at the world through windows, to look and sometimes hunger for the things she might have had. She confessed it in one of her significant poems:

> I had been hungry all the years;
> My noon had come to dine;
> I, trembling, drew the table near,
> And touched the curious wine.

'Twas this on tables I had seen,
When turning, hungry, lone,
I looked in windows, for the wealth
I could not hope to own.

I did not know the ample bread,
'Twas so unlike the crumb
The birds and I had often shared
In Nature's dining-room.

The plenty hurt me, 'twas so new,—
Myself felt ill and odd,
As berry of a mountain bush
Transplanted to the road.

Nor was I hungry; so I found
That hunger was a way
Of persons outside windows,
The entering takes away.

In her day, her birthplace, Amherst, was a small, tightly organized town. The prevailing religion was a rigid Calvinism; people went to church three times every Sunday. Emily's father was a lawyer, legislator, member of the Governor's Council, and a dominating figure in the community. He had a son and another daughter, but Emily was his favorite. She worshiped him, so much so that her whole life was governed by a "father image."

To a great extent Emily Dickinson the poet has become confused with the legend of Emily Dickinson. Different biographers offered different clues to the so-called mystery of her withdrawal from the world. They implied that a hidden love affair made her shun all outside activities, and they named different men as her secret lover.

As a girl Emily was said to have had several beaux. She was not exactly frivolous, but she was gay and quick-witted. Her earliest writings show an instinctive love for banter. Without being pretty, she was piquant. She had dark bronze-colored eyes, pale, almost transparent skin, and hair that was richly auburn.

Declining to send a photograph to someone, she described herself: "I have no picture but am small, like the wren; my hair is bold, like the chestnut burr; and my eyes, like the sherry in the glass that the guest leaves."

In her early twenties something happened which completely changed her life and transformed the living girl into a legend, a ghost that has haunted the literary world. In May, 1854, during a visit in Philadelphia, she heard a sermon by the Reverend Charles Wadsworth and fell in love with the preacher. He was forty, married, a quiet but devoted servant of God. He was probably unaware of the fervor he had roused in the heart of his shyest listener. But Emily knew at once what had happened to her.

She returned to Amherst and brooded on the spell which she could not break. Nevertheless, her mind was fixed and her heart was pledged, even though she realized that there could be nothing between her and the man she had come to adore. When she learned that the Reverend Wadsworth had received a call to a pulpit in San Francisco, she wrote:

> Parting is all we know of heaven
> And all we need of hell.

She said it explicitly and at greater length in a poem which begins painfully but calmly:

> I cannot live with you.
> It would be life.
> And life is over there,
> Behind the shelf
> The sexton keeps the key to . . .

The poem ends on a note of tragic resignation:

> So we must keep apart,
> You there, I here,
> With just the door ajar,
> That oceans are,
> And prayer,
> And that pale sustenance,
> Despair.

Almost all her love poems were written within a few years after her acceptance of a love that never could be fulfilled. The first lines of many of them reveal her anguish and her abnegation: "Who never lost are unprepared," "The heart asks pleasure first," " 'Twas a long parting," "No rack can torture me," "Of all the souls that stand create." Their burden, the refusal to love again, is condensed in twelve of her most tight-lipped lines:

> The soul selects her own society,
> Then shuts the door;
> On her divine majority
> Obtrude no more.
>
> Unmoved, she notes the chariot's pausing
> At her low gate;
> Unmoved, an emperor is kneeling
> Upon her mat.
>
> I've known her from an ample nation
> Choose one;
> Then close the valves of her attention
> Like stone.

Never before had American poetry achieved such poignant yet such controlled emotion as in Emily Dickinson's lyrics. True to the person, everything about her verse was original: the thought, the discarding of the then fashionable rhetoric, the use of unconventional and sometimes discordant rhymes and half-rhymes. All that she needed was a brief stanza or two to express the maximum of feeling with a minimum of syllables.

Emily Dickinson had kept her self to herself ever since she was twenty-five. She remained at home and alone. Her sister acted as a barrier between her and a too inquisitive community, while she withdrew more and more into a shell of solitude. She wore nothing but white. She had a few friends, but she rarely saw them; she preferred to communicate with them by letter and with bits of rhyme. She loved music but refused to come into the room where it was played, choosing to stay outside in the obscurity (or security) of the hall.

Although she wrote continually, she would not offer anything to be printed. She had a habit of jotting down her lines anywhere, on the backs of cooking recipes, on the insides of envelopes, on brown paper bags from the grocer, anything that came to hand. From time to time these scraps were tied together in little packages. After her death, her sister was confronted with what Emily had left and turned to Mrs. Todd, a neighbor who had been close to Emily, and to Colonel Higginson, a literary authority who had been asked by Emily whether her poems "breathed." Mrs. Todd and Colonel Higginson selected and published some one hundred and fifteen verses, and a year later issued another collection of one hundred and seventy-six poems. Five years later Mrs. Todd alone put together a third volume as well as a selection of letters.

The poems were not only "edited," but, in many instances, incorrectly deciphered and arbitrarily changed. The editors' taste was extremely conventional; they altered rhymes and even lines to give what they considered better "finish." Other collections of Emily Dickinson's poems—poems found in or unearthed from various places—appeared from time to time. But it was not until 1955, almost seventy years after her death, that the first complete, scrupulously edited collection was published. It was in three volumes and contained the surprising amount of seventeen hundred and seventy-five poems. It was figured out that in a single year, 1862, the year after the Reverend Wadsworth's departure to California, Emily Dickinson had written more than three hundred and fifty pathetic and impassioned poems.

In 1883 her health began to fail. She suffered from extreme nervousness. There were periods of prostration, although she maintained that "the crisis of the sorrow of many years is all that tires me." Finally, in her mid-fifties she contracted Bright's disease, and on May 15, 1886, she died in the house in which she was born.

Although everything Emily Dickinson wrote was original, all of it is by no means perfect. She was often too self-indulgent, too arch, as though the mature person was sometimes not only a child but a rather spoiled child. However, the greater part of her poetry is radiant with dazzling vision. Her themes are few— Life, Love, Nature, Eternity—yet they are enriched with an uncanny combination of observation and imagination. It is nothing less than magic that can speak of a dog's soft padding as "belated feet, like intermittent plush"; that can see a train, like some monstrous cat, "lap the miles and lick the valleys up"; that can watch a storm provoke "a strange mob of panting trees"; or observe evening, "the housewife in the west," sweep the sky "with many-colored brooms and leave the shreds behind"; or use the word "zero" to describe the sense of ultimate cold at an encounter with a snake, the feeling being "zero at the bone"; or condense within eight lines the tension of suspense:

> Elysium is as far as to
> The very nearest room,
> If in that room a friend await
> Felicity or doom.
>
> What fortitude the soul contains,
> That it can so endure
> The accent of a coming foot,
> The opening of a door.

Equally suggestive is another lyric of two stanzas. Rarely has affirmation been expressed more simply and, at the same time, more powerfully than in:

> I never saw a moor,
> I never saw the sea;
> Yet know I how the heather looks,
> And what a wave must be.
>
> I never spoke with God,
> Nor visited in Heaven;
> Yet certain am I of the spot
> As if the chart were given.

Emily Dickinson's mind was mirrored in the privacy of her work, unlike anything else in literature. She is unquestionably the most thought-compelling, the most revealing, and the most rewarding of all women poets.

Unofficial Laureate

RUDYARD KIPLING
[1865–1936]

RUDYARD KIPLING may not have been the most profound but he was the most popular poet of his day. His ardent patriotism, his glorification of everything that was English, his enthusiasm for all the wonders of the world—"for to admire an' for to see" —his unflagging gusto and zest for life, made him his country's unofficial laureate. He could, in fact, have had the laureateship; it was offered to him after the death of Tennyson. But he declined the honor, feeling he could do more for himself and the nation as an uncommitted writer.

Son of John Lockwood Kipling, who was an esteemed illustrator, and Alice MacDonald, daughter of a Wesleyan clergyman and sister-in-law of the artist Edward Burne-Jones, Rudyard Kipling was born December 30, 1865, in Bombay, India, where his father had gone to become the principal of a school of art. At the age of six the son was sent to England and came under the care of a harsh elderly relative whom he portrayed in a short story, "Baa, Baa, Black Sheep." However, he enjoyed his holidays spent in Fulham, a London borough, with Burne-Jones. At twelve he was educated at Westward Ho, a school in Devon; his experiences there are recorded in *Stalky and Co.,* a boy's story that is a mixture of kindness and cruelty, misery

213

and amusement. One of the central characters, the nearsighted, undersized Beetle, is Kipling himself.

Kipling was not quite sixteen when he returned to India and, a year later, was given a position as a subeditor of the *Civil and Military Gazette* of Lahore, where his father had become curator of the museum. He was twenty-one when his first volume appeared; it was called *Departmental Ditties* and consisted, as the title suggests, chiefly of light verse. Shortly after this debut, a more important volume was published, *Plain Tales from the Hills,* made up of the prose pieces he had contributed to the *Gazette.* Before his twenty-fourth year he was the author of six volumes including *Soldiers Three, The Phantom 'Rickshaw,* and *Wee Willie Winkie.* Although his work increased in scope and depth as he grew older, these early stories are among his finest works. Half fact and half fiction, they attained world-wide circulation.

Kipling resolved to broaden his background; he journeyed to the Orient and came back by way of the United States. The travel pieces which he sent to his paper in Lahore were collected in a book entitled *From Sea to Sea.*

By this time Kipling had become internationally famous. Readers found his narratives fascinating and his characters remarkable; they were captivated by the young author's exuberance and his amazing, seemingly magical, way of creating an exotic but convincing atmosphere for his tales.

His reputation as a storyteller was enhanced by his skill as a writer of verse. *Barrack Room Ballads* may not be poetry of the first rank—most of the poems were written in soldiers' offhand slang—but they are true ballads, racy and vigorous, exciting, often boisterous, and thoroughly enjoyable. At a time when certain poets were indicating an escape from life by painting tapestry-like pictures of a prettified past, Kipling glorified in the present. He celebrated the wonders of the modern world by acclaiming engineers, bridge-builders, seamen, stokers, soldiers. Men and women who rarely read poetry could not only read but recite by heart such poems as "Gunga Din," "Danny Deever," "Fuzzy Wuzzy," "Boots," "Mandalay," and "The Ballad of East and West" with its affirmative conclusion:

Oh, East is East and West is West, and never the twain
      shall meet,
Till Earth and Sky stand presently at God's great
      Judgment seat.
But there is neither East nor West, Border, nor Breed,
      nor Birth,
When two strong men stand face to face, though they
      come from the ends of the earth!

At twenty-seven Kipling paid another visit to the United States, where he collaborated with a writer, Wolcott Balastier, and married his sister. It is possible that Kipling might have remained in America—he settled for a while in Vermont, his wife's state—but the natives were aloof and his wife's relatives were unpleasant. After five years, during which Kipling wrote the *Jungle Books* and *Captains Courageous,* two favorites of youth which grow more endearing with age, Kipling returned to England.

He lived there quietly the rest of his life. He refused to be drawn into the life of the community. His retirement and solitude in a little Sussex village were intensified after the loss of a daughter and the death of his son during World War I. But the seclusion did not silence him. He continued to write poems and stories which, if they lacked the old heartiness, showed a new subtlety and power. Literature has been enriched with *Kim,* a romance of India seen through the eyes of the boyhood Kipling, and with *The Day's Work* and *A Diversity of Creatures,* collections which include some of his most perceptive narratives.

Kipling has been accused of a flamboyant imperialism, of banging the drum for the British Empire which assumed "the white man's burden" for "the lesser breeds." Yet this man who seemed contemptuous of any race except his own was the same man who wrote "Recessional." Composed at the time of Queen Victoria's Diamond Jubilee, "Recessional" is anything but the flag-waving poem that might have been expected for such an occasion. Instead of a vaunting chauvinism, it is a warning against national pride and the illusion of power: "Lo, all our

pomp of yesterday is one with Nineveh and Tyre!" Here are
the first three significant stanzas:

> God of our fathers, known of old,
>   Lord of our far-flung battle-line,
> Beneath whose awful hand we hold
>   Dominion over palm and pine—
> Lord God of Hosts, be with us yet,
> Lest we forget—lest we forget!
>
> The tumult and the shouting dies;
>   The captains and the kings depart:
> Still stands Thine ancient sacrifice,
>   An humble and a contrite heart.
> Lord God of Hosts, be with us yet,
> Lest we forget—lest we forget!
>
> Far-called, our navies melt away;
>   On dune and headland sinks the fire:
> Lo, all our pomp of yesterday
>   Is one with Nineveh and Tyre!
> Judge of the Nations, spare us yet,
> Lest we forget—lest we forget!

In spite of wide acclaim, Kipling declined to be turned into
a literary lion. He refused not only the laureateship but the
much prized Order of Merit, even though it was offered to him
three times. However, at forty-two he received the Nobel Prize
for Literature, and at sixty he accepted the gold medal of the
Royal Society of Literature. There followed honorary degrees
from universities in England and Europe. He was working on
his autobiography, discreetly entitled *Something of Myself,*
when he died on January 17, 1936, a few weeks after his
seventieth birthday.

Some critics have regarded Kipling as a skilled versifier rather
than an inspired—or inspiring—poet. Replying to his detractors
in an introduction to a selection of Kipling's poems, T. S. Eliot
wrote: "I can think of a number of poets who have written
great poetry, but only a very few whom I should call great verse

writers." Kipling's was unquestionably great verse. It not only played countless variations on unnumbered themes, it also probed. It penetrated the exteriors of everyday living; it revealed the marvels of machinery, the wonders of wireless communication, the minds and souls of men and women of every rank and race. Essentially a poet of and for the people, Kipling was a great storyteller and a ballad-maker whose songs were not only characteristic of his own age but for all ages.

Land of Heart's Desire

WILLIAM BUTLER YEATS

[1865-1939]

WILLIAM BUTLER YEATS, greatest of Ireland's poets, was born at Sandyhurst, near Dublin, June 13, 1865. Both his father and his brother were artists, and when the family moved to London, Yeats became an art student. His boyhood schooling had been unhappy. Dissatisfied with his classroom exercises, his teachers accused him of being a dreamer, an accusation which was not unjustified. He was not good at games; the boys made fun of his half-shy, half-haughty expression, his slight stature, his awkwardness, and his unwillingness to join them in sports. Spending most of his hours in books, he comforted himself with romantic illusions, imaginary adventures, and highly colored fantasies. He said that he began to write poetry "to find a cure for my own ailment. . . . I was humiliated, so I wrote always of proud, confident men and women."

Nearing twenty, Yeats was undecided whether he should be a painter, a poet, or an interpreter of the folk and fairy tales he had heard in Ireland. He painted hazy romantic sketches faintly reminiscent of Turner's dreamlike canvases; made a lifelong friend of another mystical painter-poet, George Russell, who signed his work with the initials AE; and, at twenty-one, published his first book, *Mosada,* a moony, melodramatic play set

218

in Morocco. He also grew interested in psychical research and Eastern philosophy. He became chairman of a group that called itself The Hermetic Society and concerned itself with such matters as the fourth dimension and unseen forces. The group was particularly occupied with theosophy, a belief that man can establish direct communication with divine principles through contemplation and revelation. When his father and friends grew alarmed that Yeats might lose touch with reality, he wrote to the Irish patriot John O'Leary, "The mystical life is the center of all that I think and all that I wrote. . . . I have always considered myself a voice of what I believe to be a greater renascence—the revolt of the soul against the intellect."

Yeats was twenty-six when he helped organize the Rhymers' Club. The club consisted not only of poets who specialized in the latest fashions (chiefly those imported from France) but also of occasional artists who contributed to *The Yellow Book* and other "advanced" publications. One of the members, Ernest Rhys, described Yeats at that time as "extremely pale and exceedingly thin, a raven lock over his forehead, his face so narrow that there was hardly room in it for his luminous black eyes." A born joiner, Yeats also associated himself with the Celtic League and became a leading figure in the Irish revival, a revival that ended in revolution. By the time he was thirty he had published six volumes of verse. Like his early paintings, most of the poems were romantically mystical, beautiful in their very vagueness. They were not only dreamily pictorial but richly musical, and the music was haunting, otherworldly, suggesting lovely landscapes lit by twilight in a land of heart's desire.

Here are two alluring lyrics of the period:

THE SONG OF WANDERING AENGUS

I went out to the hazel wood,
Because a fire was in my head,
And cut and peeled a hazel wand,
And hooked a berry to a thread;

And when white moths were on the wing,
And moth-like stars were flickering out,
I dropped the berry in a stream
And caught a little silver trout.

When I had laid it on the floor
I went to blow the fire aflame,
But something rustled on the floor,
And some one called me by my name:
It had become a glimmering girl
With apple blossoms in her hair
Who called me by my name and ran
And faded through the brightening air.

Though I am old with wandering
Through hollow lands and hilly lands,
I will find out where she has gone,
And kiss her lips and take her hands;
And walk among long dappled grass,
And pluck till time and times are done
The silver apples of the moon,
The golden apples of the sun.

THE LAKE ISLE OF INNISFREE

I will arise and go now, and go to Innisfree,
And a small cabin build there, of clay and wattles
    made;
Nine bean rows will I have there, a hive for the honey
    bee,
    And live alone in the bee-loud glade.

And I shall have some peace there, for peace comes
    dropping slow,
Dropping from the veils of the morning to where the
    cricket sings;
There midnight's all a glimmer, and noon a purple
    glow,
    And evening full of the linnet's wings.

I will arise and go now, for always night and day
I hear lake water lapping with low sounds by the shore;
While I stand on the roadway, or on the pavements
    gray,
    I hear it in the deep heart's core.

Yeats differed with his colleagues at the Rhymers' Club, yet
he attended its meetings not only for companionship but for
physical comfort. Late in life he remembered how bitter cold
London was to a poorly clad, impoverished youth, how he went
about on foot because he had no money for bus fare, how afternoon tea was not for him, as with most, a snack between lunch
and dinner but a whole meal during a time when he had little
or no nourishment.

He was in his mid-twenties when he fell violently in love
with the beautiful Maud Gonne, a heroine of the Irish nation-
alist movement. Inspired by her, Yeats wrote plays which were
not only passionate but patriotic; one of them, *Cathleen Ni
Houlihan,* an ardent allegory, was written for Maud, and Yeats
hoped she would act the chief part. When she told him that she
valued his friendship more than his love, he refused to believe
it; when he learned that she had gone to be married in Paris,
he felt as if his "ears had been deafened and the sight of his
eyes blinded with lightning." He never wholly recovered from
his devotion.

As he matured, Yeats tired of the vague enchantments of his
youth. He turned against the kind of poetry that cast its spell
by rhetorical devices. "Sentimentality is deceiving one's self,"
he said. "Rhetoric is deceiving other people." Nevertheless,
even when he abandoned his early manner and wrote in a
much plainer style, he achieved a resounding rhetoric that was
native to him, a prophetic kind of Irish oratory. In "The Second
Coming" he wrote grimly:

Things fall apart; the centre cannot hold;
Mere anarchy is loosed upon the world.
The blood-dimmed tide is loosed, and everywhere
The ceremony of innocence is drowned.

In his search for truth Yeats constantly sought for spiritual values. Experiencing a revival of his youthful interest in psychical studies, he met Georgie Hyde-Lees and found they had many things in common, including a deep concern with automatic writing and other mysterious phenomena. An engagement followed, and in his fifty-second year, Yeats married for the first time. He and his wife went to live in a tower on the Irish coast, and his work increased in richness. Many critics believe that his later poetry is not only more vigorous but also more penetrating than anything he had previously written. In the early poetry Yeats had withdrawn from the everyday world; he had hidden his face "among a crowd of starts." In the later poems he reflected "the whole man: blood, imagination, and intellect running together." The new expression was not merely a poetry of esthetic pleasure but a poetry which was to act as a "handmaid of humanity." Such poems as "Byzantium," "A Dialogue of Self and Soul," and "Among School Children" influenced a whole generation of younger poets.

Yeats was sixty-two when he was awarded the Nobel Prize for Literature. At the height of his powers, he was now hailed as a many-sided citizen of the world. He had been a playwright who had translated some of the sacred writings of the East; he had defended strikers during an employers' lockout; and he had served as a liberal senator of the Irish Free State. His three-volume autobiography—*Reveries over Childhood, The Trembling of the Veil,* and *Dramatis Personae*—which took ten years to complete, presents a fabulous figure who recreated myths and built legends about himself.

In his seventies Yeats had trouble breathing. In great pain he said that it was harder for him to live than to die. Hoping to escape the rigors of winter, he went to southern France. There, in Roquebrune, near Nice, he suffered a breakdown and died of heart failure January 28, 1939. His body was brought back and buried in Ireland.

"You Come Too"

ROBERT FROST
[1874–1963]

I'm going out to clean the pasture spring;
I'll only stop to rake the leaves away
(And wait to watch the water clear, I may);
I sha'n't be gone long.   —You come too.

I'm going out to fetch the little calf
That's standing by its mother. It's so young,
It totters when she licks it with her tongue.
I sha'n't be gone long.   —You come too.

THESE LINES are typical of the tone which won so many
admirers for Robert Frost. The simple surface makes the poem
seem ordinary, and ordinary it is in the sense of being forthright, familiar, and immediately understood. Ordinary was an
adjective Robert Frost never resented, for he was no less the
ordinary man for being so extraordinary an artist. His is a
poetry of persuasion; the stanzas above stand at the beginning
of his collected poems. They are called "The Pasture" and
they act as an invitation, an appeal to the reader, bidding him
to accompany the poet and, with him, to explore his world. It
is expressed in the tone of conversation, of common-sense
speech, but as we go along with this poet, common sense turns
into a sense of wonder.

Robert Frost's ancestors were New Englanders of Scottish-English descent. His mother, a schoolteacher, would have remained in New England had it not been for her husband, who went to the West Coast to work on a newspaper. Their son was born in San Francisco, California, on March 26, 1874, and was christened Robert Lee Frost.

The San Francisco of Frost's boyhood was a rough town. Westerners carried revolvers as casually as easterners carried canes. Frost's father enjoyed the reckless life of a journalist-politician, but his health gave way beneath the strain. When he died of tuberculosis, he was only thirty-four, and the ten-year-old Robert was brought back to New England.

He went back to poverty. His mother could barely support herself, her son, and her daughter, Jean. As early as twelve, Robert had to learn living the hard way. After school hours he picked up a little money as a helper on a farm. At thirteen he worked in a shoe factory. At sixteen he pushed wagons in a textile mill. At eighteen he tended dynamos and trimmed carbon lamps over spinning machines. With his mother's help he managed to get his lessons done; when he graduated from the Lawrence, Massachusetts, High School, he delivered the valedictory. His co-valedictorian was a shy, extremely pretty girl, Elinor White. Three years later he married her.

Long before he was eighteen he knew what he wanted to be. He wanted to be a poet and—although everyone laughed at the idea—earn a livelihood by poetry alone. He was nineteen when a magazine, *The Independent,* accepted a poem and paid him fifteen dollars for it. It was an auspicious start. Frost hoped he could now depend on poems as a source of income. But it was years before his hope was realized. The other magazines were not nearly as independent as *The Independent.* They favored the overdecorated, dulcet, prettified verse-making of the period. Frost's unstylish style, his plain-speaking poetry, so full of stripped truths, was not to their taste; it did not seem like poetry at all. It was obvious that he had to occupy himself with something more financially rewarding in order to take care of a family.

He turned from one occupation to another. He ran a newspaper column. He wrote stories about the countryside and articles for poetry journals. When he developed a persistent cough and the doctor learned that Frost's father had died of tuberculosis, he was advised to find outdoor work. Not too happily but determinedly, Frost became a farmer.

He tried college—twice. He had gone to Dartmouth, where he stayed only a year, and later to Harvard, where he stuck it out for two years. He could not discipline himself to the curriculum and the academic routine. It is an irony that the poet who, during the last part of his life, was presented with dozens of honorary degrees never stayed in college long enough to receive his diploma.

Frost's face reflected his background. His features seemed carved out of native granite; his eyes were the palest but clearest blue; his mouth was both prim and puckish with an underlip that looked bee-stung. His bones appeared to be loosely hung, and his voice never lost its down-east twang, the accent of a resolute countryman.

He was not fond of farming—his farm had such poor soil that he said he had to blast rocks in order to plant potatoes. He struggled with it for ten years. The acres yielded nothing more profitable than a crop of poetry. It was a crop that had no buyers. Finally he decided he could never be a successful farmer. With what little money he had been able to scrape up, he left New England and, nearing forty, took his growing family abroad.

In 1912 Frost settled in rural Beaconsfield, England, stubbornly tried farming again, and discovered that his English neighbors were poets. One of them, Edward Thomas, was so charmed by the newcomer that he became his dear friend and, strongly influenced by his work, dedicated his first volume of poetry to Frost. Frost himself was still without a published book. One day he looked over what he had written during twenty years. He has always admired "Invictus" and other poems by W. E. Henley and, without asking anyone to act as a go-between, decided to send his manuscript to Henley's publisher. The publisher's widow read the work of the then unknown poet and published it. Inspiring young authors impatient for publication might remember that Frost had to wait more than twenty years from the time his first verse appeared in a magazine to the time of his first book. When *A Boy's Will* appeared, Frost was thirty-eight years old.

A Boy's Will is a lyrical collection, full of reminiscences of the poet's youth. *North of Boston,* which was issued a year later, consists chiefly of unrhymed monologues and dramatic dialogues, literally a book of people. It was an instant success. When the First World War drove Frost out of England and he returned to the United States, he was already a famous man. From then on he was celebrated wherever he went. He was esteemed as though he were a classic bard, recognized as a provocative though informal teacher, appreciated as a sage who became an elder statesman, an "unacknowledged legislator." (When honor after honor descended upon him, he said he was being smothered by degrees.) Awarded the coveted Pulitzer Prize, he was the only author to win it four times. He was also the only poet who ever read a poem at the inauguration of a President, an event which took place when he recited "The Gift Outright" at President Kennedy's inauguration in 1961.

THE GIFT OUTRIGHT

The land was ours before we were the land's.
She was our land more than a hundred years
Before we were her people. She was ours
In Massachusetts, in Virginia;
But we were England's, still colonials,
Possessing what we still were unpossessed by,
Possessed by what we now no more possessed.
Something we were withholding made us weak
Until we found out that it was ourselves
We were withholding from our land of living,
And forthwith found salvation in surrender.
Such as we were we gave ourselves outright
(The deed of gift was many deeds of war)
To the land vaguely realizing westward,
But still unstoried, artless, unenhanced,
Such as she was, such as she would become.

Frost's eighty-eighth birthday was marked by three major occurrences. He received the rarely awarded Congressional Medal at a White House ceremony. He was guest of honor at a dinner attended by two hundred notables at the Pan American Union in Washington. His ninth volume of poetry, *In the Clearing,* his first collection in fifteen years, was a phenomenal financial as well as critical success: over one hundred thousand copies were sold within a few months.

By this time Frost had added to the language lines which had the trenchant quality of folklore. Readers were quick to pick up such sayings as "Something there is that doesn't love a wall" and its opposite, "Good fences make good neighbors"; chores were "doing things over and over that just won't stay done"; home was defined by a rather bitter man as "the place where, when you have to go there, they have to take you in," and by his tenderhearted wife as "something you somehow haven't to deserve."

Frost ignored reviews and articles about his work; he was annoyed when forced to face analyses of certain of his poems. He was irritated at "explanations" of his lyrics, especially one of the simplest, "Stopping by Woods on a Snowy Evening." "The trouble with this sort of criticism," he said, "is that it analyzes the poem to death. It depersonalizes the simple idea, distorts the feeling, and finally destroys whatever poetry is left in the poem. These 'interpreters' try to find symbols in everything, symbols that the poet never knew were there. Symbolism can be as bad as an embolism—it can clog up and kill a poem just as it can kill a person. That little poem means just what it says, and it says just what it means, nothing less, but nothing more."

This is the poem:

STOPPING BY WOODS ON A SNOWY EVENING

Whose woods these are I think I know.
His house is in the village though;
He will not see me stopping here
To watch his woods fill up with snow.

My little horse must think it queer
To stop without a farmhouse near
Between the woods and frozen lake
The darkest evening of the year.

He gives his harness bells a shake
To ask if there is some mistake.
The only other sound's the sweep
Of easy wind and downy flake.

The woods are lovely, dark and deep,
But I have promises to keep,
And miles to go before I sleep,
And miles to go before I sleep.

The miles Frost had to go before he could sleep were long, hard miles. His first son lived only three years. His wife, Elinor, on whom he depended for so much, died of a heart attack in her mid-fifties. His sister Jean had been confined to a state hospital for the insane and had died there. His favorite daughter had succumbed to a childbirth infection. Another daughter was mentally disturbed and had to be cared for in various "homes." His only surviving son had committed suicide. Yet, struck with one tragedy after another, Frost never complained; there is no self-pity in anything he wrote. Afflictions, he said, "must be kept down under the surface where the great griefs belong."

In his eighties Frost suffered pains in various parts of his body. In late 1962 he entered a Boston hospital to undergo surgery. The operation was successful, but blood clots settled in his lungs. His vitality kept him alive for several weeks, but on January 29, 1963, a pulmonary embolism stopped his breathing. Had he lived a little more than another year he would have been ninety years old.

Frost had many memorable things to say about poetry. He liked to say that a living poem begins its life "with a lump in the throat—a home-sickness or a love-sickness. It is a reaching-out toward expression, an effort to find fulfillment. A complete poem is one where an emotion has found its thought, and the thought has found the words." At another time he said, "For me the initial delight in poetry is in the surprise of remembering something I had forgotten, or remembering something I didn't know I knew." He never ceased to wonder at the way a straightforward meter could make a tune that could be either gay or sad, mild or wild, playful yet profound.

The pleasures of poetry are manifold. But the chief pleasure of poetry is that it lives and grows in the responsive mind. Perhaps Frost said it best in a single sentence when he defined a true poem as something which transforms both the reader and itself. "It begins," he wrote, "in delight and ends in wisdom."

It is a definition that can stand.

FOR FURTHER READING

FOR THOSE who would like further details about the lives and works of the twenty-five poets included in this volume, the following books are recommended.

GEOFFREY CHAUCER

Chaucer by G. K. Chesterton. Farrar & Rinehart, Inc., 1932.
Geoffrey Chaucer of England by Marchette Chute. E. P. Dutton & Co., Inc., 1946.
Chaucer's World compiled by Edith Rickert. Columbia University Press (paperback), 1964.

SIR PHILIP SIDNEY

Sidney's Arcadia by Walter R. Davis and Richard A. Lanham. Yale University Press, 1965.
Sidney's Poetry by David Kalstone. Harvard University Press, 1965.

WILLIAM SHAKESPEARE

Shakespeare by Mark Van Doren. Henry Holt & Co., 1939.
The Art and Life of William Shakespeare by Hazelton Spencer. Harcourt, Brace & Co., 1940.
An Introduction to Shakespeare by Marchette Chute. E. P. Dutton & Co., Inc., 1951.
An Approach to Shakespeare by D. A. Traversi. Doubleday Anchor Book (paperback), Doubleday & Co., Inc., 1956.
Shakespeare: A Biography by Peter Quennell. The World Publishing Co., 1963.

JOHN DONNE

John Donne: A Study in Discord by Hugh I'Anson Fausset. Harcourt, Brace & Co., 1924.
A Garland for John Donne edited by Theodore Spencer. Harvard University Press, 1931.
John Donne by K. W. Grandsire. Longmans, Green & Co., 1954.

ROBERT HERRICK

The Love Poems of Robert Herrick and John Donne edited and with an Introduction by Louis Untermeyer. Rutgers University Press, 1948.
Two Gentlemen: The Lives of George Herbert and Robert Herrick by Marchette Chute. E. P. Dutton & Co., 1959.

JOHN MILTON

John Milton, Englishman by James Holly Hanford. Crown Publishers, 1949.
John Milton by Kenneth Muir. Longmans, Green & Co., 1955.
Milton and the English Mind by F. E. Hutchinson. Collier Books (paperback), 1962.

ALEXANDER POPE

Pope: Poetry and Prose, with essays by Johnson, Coleridge, Hazlitt, et al., edited by H. V. D. Dyson. Oxford University Press, 1933.
Alexander Pope: A Biography by Edith Sitwell. Penguin Books (paperback), 1948.
The Pleasures of Pope selected and introduced by Peter Quennell. Pantheon Books, 1950.

WILLIAM BLAKE

William Blake the Man by Charles Gardner. E. P. Dutton & Co., 1919.
William Blake in This World by Harold Bruce. Harcourt, Brace & Co., 1925.
William Blake by Osbert Burdett. The Macmillan Co., 1926.
An Introduction to the Study of Blake by Max Plowman. J. M. Dent & Sons, Ltd., 1927.

ROBERT BURNS

Life of Burns by John Stuart Blackie. Walter Scott, Publishers (London), 1888.
Robert Burns by David Daiches. Rinehart & Co., 1950.
Robert Burns: The Man, His Work, the Legend by Maurice Lindsay. MacGibbon & Kee (London), 1954.

WILLIAM WORDSWORTH

The First Romantics (Wordsworth, Coleridge, and Southey) by Malcolm Elwin. Longmans, Green & Co., 1948.
Wordsworth. Seven Essays in Reappraisal edited by Gilbert T. Dunklin. Princeton University Press, 1951.
Wordsworth: A Reinterpretation by F. W. Bateson. Longmans, Green & Co., 1954.

SAMUEL TAYLOR COLERIDGE

The First Romantics (Wordsworth, Coleridge, and Southey) by Malcolm Elwin. Longmans, Green & Co., 1948.
The Road to Xanadu by John Livingston Lowes. Houghton Mifflin Co., 1927.
The Sacred River: Coleridge's Theory of the Imagination by James Volant Baker. Louisiana State University Press, 1960.

GEORGE GORDON, LORD BYRON

Byron: The Years of Fame by Peter Quennell. St. James Library, Collins (London), 1950.
Byron in Italy by Peter Quennell. St. James Library, Collins (London), 1951.
The Last Attachment: The Story of Byron and Teresa Guiccioli by Iris Origo. Charles Scribner's Sons, 1949.

PERCY BYSSHE SHELLEY

Portrait of Shelley by Newman Ivey White. Alfred A. Knopf, 1945.
The Young Shelley by Kenneth Neill Cameron. The Macmillan Co., 1950.
Shelley: A Life Story by Edmund Blunden. Oxford University Press (paperback), 1965.

JOHN KEATS

Keats and the Daemon King by Werner W. Beyer. Oxford University Press, 1947.

John Keats: The Living Year by Robert Gittings. Harvard University Press, 1954.

John Keats: The Making of a Poet by Aileen Ward. The Viking Press, 1963.

WILLIAM CULLEN BRYANT

William Cullen Bryant. A biographical introduction by Richard Henry Stoddard in *Poetical Works.* Houghton Mifflin Co., 1903.

ELIZABETH BARRETT BROWNING
AND ROBERT BROWNING

Robert Browning by G. K. Chesterton. The Macmillan Co., 1905.

Robert Browning: a Portrait by Betty Miller. Charles Scribner's Sons, 1953.

A Browning Handbook by William Clyde DeVane. Appleton-Century-Crofts, Inc., 1955.

Andromeda in Wimpole Street. The Love Story of Elizabeth Barrett and Robert Browning Through Extracts from Their Letters, by Dormer Creston. Eyre & Spottiswoode (London), 1950.

HENRY WADSWORTH LONGFELLOW

Young Longfellow by Lawrance Thompson. The Macmillan Co., 1938.

Longfellow: His Life and Work by Newton Arvin. Little, Brown & Co., 1963.

EDGAR ALLAN POE

Israfel: The Life and Times of Edgar Allan Poe (two volumes) by Hervey Allen. George H. Doran Co., 1926.

Edgar Allan Poe. A one-volume edition of tales, essays, articles, and poems, selected and with a biographical introduction by Philip Van Doren Stern. The Viking Press, 1945.

Edgar Allan Poe: The Man Behind the Legend by Edward Wagenknecht. Oxford University Press, 1963.

ALFRED, LORD TENNYSON

Tennyson: His Art and Relation to Modern Life by Stopford A. Brooke. G. P. Putnam's Sons, 1903.
Tennyson: A Modern Portrait by Hugh I'Anson Fausett. Appleton-Century-Crofts, Inc., 1923.

WALT WHITMAN

Whitman: An Interpretation in Narrative by Emory Holloway. Alfred A. Knopf, 1926.
Whitman by Newton Arvin. The Macmillan Co., 1938.
American Giant: Walt Whitman and His Times by Frances Winwar. Harper & Bros., 1941.
Walt Whitman: An American by Henry Seidel Canby. Houghton Mifflin Co., 1943.

EMILY DICKINSON

This Was a Poet: A Critical Biography of Emily Dickinson by George Frisbie Whicher. Charles Scribner's Sons, 1938.
Emily Dickinson's Poetry: Stairway of Surprise by Charles R. Anderson. Holt, Rinehart & Winston, 1960.
Emily Dickinson: A Collection of Critical Essays edited by Richard B. Sewall. Prentice Hall, Inc., (paperback), 1963.

RUDYARD KIPLING

Something of Myself by Rudyard Kipling. Doubleday & Co., 1937.

WILLIAM BUTLER YEATS

Autobiographies by W. B. Yeats. Macmillan & Co. (London), 1955.
Yeats: The Man and the Masks by Richard Ellmann. The Macmillan Co., 1948.
The Lonely Tower: Studies in the Poetry of W. B. Yeats by T. R. Henn. Pellegrini & Cudahy, 1952.

ROBERT FROST

Robert Frost: The Trail by Existence by Elizabeth Shepley Sergeant. Holt, Rinehart & Winston, 1960.

Robert Frost: A Collection of Critical Essays edited by James M. Cox. Prentice-Hall, Inc. (paperback), 1962.

The Letters of Robert Frost to Louis Untermeyer edited and with a running commentary by Louis Untermeyer. Holt, Rinehart & Winston, 1963.

INDEX

ABOUT THE AUTHOR

Poet, biographer and critic, Louis Untermeyer is also America's most creative anthologist. His *Treasury of Great Poems,* now in its ninth printing, was followed by the highly successful *A Treasury of Laughter.* His collections of *Modern American Poetry* and *Modern British Poetry* have sold over a million copies and are standard textbooks in schools and colleges. He has introduced more poets to readers and more readers to poetry than any other American.

Born in New York City, he was unable to comprehend geometry and consequently failed to graduate from high school. He taught himself music, art and literature while earning his living in the family's jewelry-manufacturing establishment. Nearing forty, he quit his desk at the factory, went to Europe and subsequently returned home to devote his time to writing and lecturing. He became poet-in-residence at various universities, writer for the Office of War Information, editor of the Armed Services Editions and, after World War II, editor for a leading record company. By the time he was sixty he was the author or compiler of some sixty volumes, including a novel, several travel books and stories for young people. He was appointed Consultant in Poetry at the Library of Congress for two years and was sent by the State Department to India, where he represented the United States at cultural conferences in New Delhi and Bombay.

He spends most of his time in a 240-year-old cottage in Connecticut with his wife, Bryna Ivens, a former magazine editor, surrounded by three large cats and one very small dog.

Bygones, his autobiography, was published in 1965 on his eightieth birthday.

THIS BOOK WAS SET IN

BASKERVILLE AND PALATINO TYPES BY

MARYLAND LINOTYPE COMPOSITION CO.

IT WAS PRINTED BY

HALLIDAY LITHOGRAPH CORP.

AND BOUND BY

MONTAUK BOOK MANUFACTURING CO., INC.

TYPOGRAPHY AND DESIGN ARE BY

LARRY KAMP AND BARBARA LIMAN.